The God Who Reigns

The God Who Reigns

Experiencing God's power in our lives

DON WILLIAMS

MARSHALL PICKERING

Marshall Morgan and Scott
Marshall Pickering
34–42 Cleveland Street, London W1P 5FB U.K.

Copyright © 1989 Don Williams
First published in the USA by Vine Books, Servant Publications, Ann Arbor, Michigan.

First published in the UK in 1989 by Marshall Morgan and Scott Publications Ltd
Part of the Marshall Pickering Holdings Group

All rights reserved. No part of this publication may be reproduced, stored in a retrieval system, or transmitted, in any form or by any means, electronic mechanical, photocopying, recording or otherwise, without the permission in writing, of the publisher.

Passages from Scripture used in this work have been taken from the New American Standard Bible, © 1960, 1962, 1963, 1968, 1971, 1972, 1973, 1975, 1977 by the Lockman Foundation. Used by permission.

ISBN: 0 551 01932 8

Printed in Great Britain by Cox & Wyman Ltd, Reading

Table of Contents

Forewords   vii
Preface   xiii

1. God Is King, But Do We Know It?   1
2. The Reign of God   23
3. Recovering the Christian Mind   33
4. The Assault of Satan   51
5. The Kingdom Revealed, Rejected, and Restored   63
6. Kingdom Power   79
7. A Future and a Hope   93
8. The Kingdom Come: The Ministry of Jesus   105
9. Imitators of Christ: The Ministry of the Church   123
10. Come, Lord Jesus   143

Chapter Notes   153

Forewords

BACK IN 1983 Don Williams attended an evening worship session of the Anaheim Vineyard Christian Fellowship. He had heard about the Vineyard from a Fuller Seminary student who was enrolled in an experimental course at the School of World Mission, Fuller Seminary, in Pasadena, California, that I was teaching under the supervision of C. Peter Wagner. The course, carrying the catalog number MC:510, was called "Signs, Wonders, and Church Growth." I didn't know it at the time, but Don was on a quest for the healing power of Jesus.

Don was touched by the worship that Sunday evening, and he returned the next week and introduced himself to me. I immediately saw in Don a man with a heart for God. However, as a Princeton educated New Testament scholar, seminary professor, and Presbyterian pastor he was quite skeptical about anything supernatural.

Don thought he merely needed solid biblical teaching to be convinced that divine healing was for today. But I knew better. He was in need of a worldview shift, in which he would allow for the active reign of God to break into his life and, through him, into the lives of others. Of course, he needed solid teaching, but he also needed a *demonstration* of God's power today—beginning with healing in his own life. So I embraced him, inviting him to accompany me as I went out on ministry trips. He accepted.

At first he sat back analyzing everything I said and did, trying to make sense of my attempts not only to talk about healing but actually pray for the sick. Soon he was pulled in by the move of the Holy Spirit. First he had a dramatic experience of God's power, then he began praying for others with effectiveness. He's never been the same since: a theologian and pastor who lives what he teaches and writes about. He no longer excludes the possibility of God's kingdom breaking into any part of his life!

One issue that hasn't changed for Don is that he is still very much a man of the Book. His concern, as he so aptly communicates it in *The God Who Reigns,* is that we live out a central theme of Scripture: that God is King, and that we are called into a kingdom where God reigns directly and dynamically in our lives. The establishment of the kingdom of God in our thinking and practice removes any bias to the miraculous—and we are then in a position to be changed by God's direct intervention in our lives.

This book could have just as easily been titled *A Theology of Signs and Wonders,* for it develops the biblical thinking behind the supernatural working of God in the world today. But don't be put off by the word "theology"; what Don writes isn't dead theology. It's alive and pregnant with the kingdom of God and practical application for how God reigns today. Read it prayerfully and fearfully, for if you believe what Don writes, you'll never be the same.

JOHN WIMBER
Anaheim, California

A YEAR OR TWO AGO I walked into an auditorium where Don Williams was getting launched on a description of what he referred to as "the theology of the Third Wave." As I sat down I was startled to hear him refer to me and to express misgiving because his address followed mine. He need not have worried. The congregation laughed during my address. They were electrified during Don's.

And rightly so. I had looked forward to listening to what he had to say, even though I had heard the address before, and as I listened excitement set my pulse racing just as it had the first time. It was not his oratory that enthralled me (though that was exhilarating enough) but the truths he so clearly and forcefully stated. Don proclaimed what my mind and my spirit both cried out to hear—truths whose day had come. This book elaborated the thinking that went into his address.

Theology is about God, in whom professional theologians take a professional interest. They tend to belong to one of two groups. Some are fascinated by abstract God-ideas, but others are excited about God himself. Don (who might not wish to call himself a theologian but who thinks like one) belongs to the latter group. It is the King who excites him. The kingdom enthralls him because of the King who rules it. And this is as it should be.

I am, like most Christians, an amateur theologian. Like the professionals I am tempted to re-create God in my own image, making of him what one theologian called "the sort of God with whom I can be comfortable." Few of us have the honesty to express it that way, yet most of us do it without even realizing what we are doing. Theologians (whether amateur or professional) are influenced in their thinking by their unconscious biases, even though they try not to be.

We rationalize. That is to say we (conservatives and charismatics, liberals and fundamentalists, Catholics and Protestants, sacramentalists and "low church" ers) reinterpret the Bible to accommodate it either to our own experience or else to our lack of it. Not only do we rationalize, we *react*. Too frequently our theologizings represent a reaction to what we perceive as dangerous error. And in reacting we commonly over-react, flinging living babies away with dirty bath water.

We wear psychological spectacles as we study the Bible. We see what pleases us. Sooner or later we explain away what bothers us—or else we never see it in the first place. God has to grab us by the scruff of the neck to shake us out of our complacency, or we would eternally wander in an epistemological morass.

Fundamentalist theology of the twentieth century, initially a valuable reaffirmation of faith in the face of liberal theology, gradually took on the coloring not only of a reaction against liberals but against the Pentecostal movement. In so doing it not only became more reactionary, but it threw out the baby of God's power, all the while denying that it was doing so. And the reaction at that point was less a reflection of biblical truth than of unconscious fears blinding us to some things Scripture was saying.

Don Williams is keenly aware of our being victims of imperfect minds, and quotes Timothy Leary, "Reason is a tissue-thin artifact easily destroyed by a slight alteration of the body's chemistry." But the day came when he realized that he was a victim of the worldview imparted to him by his heritage and his education—a worldview designed to keep fear at bay. His theological education had given him "a system of doctrine with which to control my faith, exegetical tools with which to control the Bible, management tools with which to control the church, and counseling tools with which to control people."

Some schools of theology are fearful of experience. For them arguments illustrated by personal experience are suspect. Better to confine ourselves to the sterility of abstractions than to sink in the treacherous quicksand of our subjective passions. Now it is true that only valid experiences given by God validate a truth. What validates is not experience itself, but the nature and content of a specific experience.

In the real world experiences often validate truth. Biblical writers affirm the truths they present by describing their experiences. Isaiah tells the awesome story of his subjectively experienced call to be a prophet, as do Jeremiah and Ezekiel. Jesus himself tells Nicodemus " . . . we speak of what we know, and we testify to what we have seen . . ." Peter assured us that we do not follow cunningly devised fables, but the result of first hand observation. Paul makes the same kind of reference to the gospel revealed to him in Arabia as the prophets. Ordinary people call experience to validate truth also. The Samaritan prostitute, *on the basis of her experience of him*, cries, "Is not this the Christ?" And throughout the history of the Church, God repeatedly gives people the experience of being taken up by scruff of the neck as he shakes them and says, "Wake up! Let's get back to basics!"

This is what happened to Don Williams. In presenting his book, he describes the experiences which tore him out of the straight-jacket of reactionary theology, a theology that had bound and emasculated him, setting him free by sovereign power.

Refinements in theology come as we wake up to what we have flung away in our zeal against error, and Don Williams' book represents such a refinement. But it is refinement brought about by the rescue of a living baby, a rejected baby Moses so to speak, one God has decided to preserve for his own sovereign purposes.

There has never really been a satisfactory theology of power to show us where God's power fits into the Church's role in history. Kingdom theology provides a vehicle for such an understanding. God's power resides in who and what he is. He is King. He is Supreme Governor. He rules over all, and that rule extends to the history of our planet. He rules in subtle ways we are scarcely aware of, and also in dramatic ways.

Throughout biblical history he broke in on our time-space continuum repeatedly, turning the sun back, opening a dry path in the sea, sending his own fire to consume a sacrifice, and opening a way through death. And he has not finished. God is King and he does not intend to abdicate. He will continue to give signs and wonders as he sees fit.

But he likes to do so through people. He calls on us to remember who and what he is, to repent of our arrogant need to see ourselves in charge of his church, and of trying to confine him inside the cage of our limited thoughts about him. For he is a mighty God about to do a new thing. And in sovereign grace he wishes to do it with all who will trust and obey him.

John White

Preface

THIS BOOK COMES OUT OF A DEEP CONVICTION that God is restoring an understanding of his kingdom both theologically and experientially in his church today. Moreover, I am convinced that the kingdom provides the biblical key to the Pentecostal experience, the charismatic renewal, and the "Third Wave" awakening which have influenced Christian life so dramatically and accelerated the tempo of world evangelism. I also believe that our grasp of the kingdom will hold these movements on a proper biblical course.

The dynamic work of the Holy Spirit is causing much theological ferment. For example, David Hubbard, the President of Fuller Theological Seminary, writes in the foreword to a faculty study entitled *Ministry and the Miraculous,* "I would like to think of this book as the first fruits of a harvest of discussion on these issues [such as healing] which are as crucial as they are delicate" (p. 19). Indeed, I will continue the "harvest of discussion" here as I interact and take issue with many of this study's conclusions.

As the reader will see in chapter one, this book comes out of my own personal journey into renewal. I cannot write it without profound gratitude to those who nurtured me in my evangelical faith. These include especially Jim Rayburn, the founder of Young Life, Dr. Henrietta C. Mears, Dr. Bill Bright, the Rev. Earl Palmer, the Rev. Don Moomaw, Dr. F. Dale Bruner, and my pastor and friend for ten years, Dr. Raymond I. Lindquist. Keith Miller and Lloyd Ogilvie gave me healthy models of renewal in the context of the relational theology movement. I am also indebted beyond measure for my knowledge of biblical theology to Professors Otto Piper and James Martin of Princeton and, above all, to my doctoral advisor, W.D. Davies of Union Seminary and now emeritus at Duke University.

A surprising turn in the road brought me into contact with John Wimber, the founder of the Vineyard Christian Fellowship in Anaheim, California, in 1983. This led me into a whole new direction in ministry and a reformulation of its biblical basis. John became my pastor and friend for this current phase of my pilgrimage. He also gave me the opportunity to lecture at several major conferences and encouraged me to write the results which now make up this study. At the same time, Francis MacNutt became a dear friend, and his teaching in the area of healing ministry has had a major influence upon my life. I cannot also help but mention others who have been special to me for this leg of the journey. They include: Mark Slomka, Mark McCoy, Tommy Andrews, Peter Kenvin, Anita Speier, Bill Gerrity, Ron Rimmer, Eddie Feuer, and Dr. Joe Ozawa. I also am deeply indebted to Bob and Nancy Hunt, Kevin Springer, Ann Spangler, and Beth Nethery without whom this book would have not seen the light of day.

Most of all, in this life, I am grateful for my wife Kathryn; her love, companionship, sacrifice, encouragement, and faith kept me going to the end. The flaws here are mine. The glory goes to the one, great sovereign King whose kingdom is come and coming.

ONE

God Is King, But Do We Know It?

GOD IS KING. HE REIGNS ENTHRONED in glory with a sea of flaming angels bowing low before him and rising to shout his praises. From his throne he speaks and the galaxies are hurled into space. From his throne he orders the molten, gaseous stars, and directs the planets circling them. From his throne he places our earth into its orbit and rules the ages of our geological and historical life. From his throne he upholds all things and judges all things. Moreover, on the awesome final day each of us will stand before his throne and give an account of our lives to him.

Beyond our current chaos, the razor edge of nuclear night upon which we stand, beyond Northern Ireland, the Gaza Strip, Ethiopia, Haiti, Nicaragua, Afghanistan, and a hundred other wounds which seep nightly from our TV screens, and beyond our own personal anxieties, our deep loneliness when the lights go out at night, beyond all of this stands the eternal, supernatural, divine kingdom, pulsating with power, revealing God's glory.

This kingdom is not merely some otherworldly hope, Marx's opiate for the masses, or a spiritual "high" reached by mystical moments of mindless chanting. The shattering, life-changing news of the Bible is that the King who rules this kingdom both sustains our world from heaven and decisively and irrevocably invades it in the incarnation of his Son who bears his dynamic Spirit. What this means for us is that our lives can and must be changed now. While we may routinely pray, "Thy kingdom come, Thy will be done on earth as it is in heaven," God is actually answering this prayer throughout our world as he manifests his kingdom reign. Thus, he is releasing his Holy Spirit in power, opening hearts to his lively presence, healing wounds past and present, breaking compulsive, addictive behavior, and elevating the poor into his presence by expelling our present darkness and recreating our fallen humanity. We have the unique opportunity to experience this kingdom by faith and to see it personally intersect our lives before we are catapulted into eternity where both faith and unbelief will become sight, either to our joy or to our horror.

Since God is King and his kingdom is here for us, we no longer have to spread a religious veneer over the sadness of our deep-rooted unbelief. We no longer have to carry the guilt of our sexual misadventures. We no longer have to try to control our lives, grasping onto people and possessions with an infantile fist, afraid that if we let them go we will be alone in an empty universe. Since God is King and we will account for our lives before him, our lives have eternal meaning. Death neither blanks out our consciousness nor releases us back to earth in a continuing cycle of reincarnation. Our "yes" or "no" before God determines our final destiny. As T.S. Eliot remarks,

> [The possibility of damnation] is so immense a relief in a world of electoral reform, plebiscites, sex reform and dress reform, that damnation itself is an immediate form of salvation—of salvation from the ennui of modern life, because it at last gives some significance to living.

Thus, it is of the utmost urgency that we understand God and respond to his kingdom. The theme of this book is no "trivial pursuit." It needs to be at the top of our agenda for life and we need to study it substantially rather than superficially since the God of the Bible is the real God, Creator, Redeemer, and Judge, and there is no other.

Now, I ask honestly, is this the God whom we worship? Or is ours a "lesser god?" Perhaps he is a kind but impotent old man who merely keeps his eye on us. He may be a lurking truant officer waiting for us to cut class or the distant "Chairman of the Board" of the church corporation which we manage in his name. Perhaps our God is an affirming pop-psychologist who puts up with our bad habits and reminds us that we're okay. If these are our images of him, no wonder that the church is in disrepair. I have sat in the privacy of my office with heroin addicts who mask their needle tracts with tatoos, sexually abused children who pay for their rape with anorexia and bulimia, homosexuals consumed with lust who cry out for love, couples whose marriages have spawned "buyers' remorse," AIDS patients with icy fear encircling their hearts. Faced with this pain over the years I have often asked myself, "How can I possibly bear the burden of these broken, hungry people who have found their way to me?" And deeper still, "How can I bear their burden when I admit (in a moment of candor) that I carry many of the same things as well?" "Physician heal thyself!" No wonder there is such a despairing exodus of pastors and priests from our churches today. No wonder sensitive souls turn to psychology, social work, or political action for answers. Here, they conclude, at least some tangible good can be done amidst the enveloping darkness. However, our longing is for more than this. Whether we know it or not, we long for the kingdom of God.

I must confess that after being a Christian for over thirty-five years, I have only recently begun to see the God of the Bible clearly as the mighty King who invades both this world and my life in order to establish his reign and bring all things under submission to him. For too long I have worshiped a "lesser god" whom I (and most of the church) have shaped to fit our secular perception of reality, our man-centered vision and limited, rational mind-set. Let me explain.

While Jesus' disciples were ready to be bloodied rather than to worship the emperor, we have allowed ourselves to be seduced by the gods of our age, to worship humanism and skepticism. As a result, scholars have rationalized, allegorized, or demythologized the Bible. Rather than holding that Jesus walked on the water, they suppose that he walked on a sandbar, creating an illusion for his followers. Or, better still, the Gospel writers themselves fantasized his walking on the water for "theological" reasons, symbolizing his transcendence over nature or his triumph over the watery chaos of our existence in this world. In light of this, it would be hard to deny that most Western Christians have sold out intellectually to the secular culture and, therefore, have little expectation that God will work directly and dynamically in our churches and in our personal lives. As a result, we are exhorted to assent to abstract biblical truths without welcoming the descent of the living God into our midst where most of us live with unhealed brokenness and pain behind our Sunday masks.

The sting of this diagnosis is that as a "solid evangelical," I too have tried to reason away the supernatural acts of God as moral ideals or disembodied "spiritual truths." While confident that Jesus is real and that the Bible is the Word of God, I have been tempted to separate my spiritual life from the rest of my thoughts and behavior. For some years I have agreed with Francis Schaeffer that modern theology, by its skepticism toward biblical records of creation and history, tends to kick faith into a disembodied "upper storey" unrelated to both.[1] Supernatural, biblical events didn't really happen, they are only good stories about what is ideally true, and this ideal exists in the upper storey of our heads, not in the lower storey of our experience. To be sure, I militantly refused to join the modern theologians at this point. Thus, I would never have denied that Jesus actually performed miracles. However, I believed that his casting out demons and healing the sick were proofs of his diety rather than essential aspects of his ministry. What I failed to see was that my modern perception of reality did exactly what Schaeffer warned against.

Intellectually, I had faith that God exercised his supernatural power; nevertheless, I did not have faith that I could experience his power in my life. The idea that as his disciple I too was to cast out demons and heal the sick in Jesus' name was beyond my comprehension.

Like many Christians, I had been taught not to expect any powerful work of the Holy Spirit after conversion, and I believed that the gifts of tongues, miracles, and prophecy ceased with the closing of the Apostolic Age. Therefore, I concluded that signs and wonders proved theology to a primitive, unlettered generation. My college classmates needed apologetics, "evidence that demands a verdict," I supposed, rather than God's direct intervention in their lives. While embracing a biblical, supernatural perception of reality intellectually, most of my life was lived without any daily experience of it. My education and experience proved that the critical power of my mind could control my world. When I prayed for God's guidance, I expected it to come through my intellectual comprehension of the Bible (from which I prooftexted many decisions), as well as through wise counsel, and life's circumstances. There would be no angels, visions, or divine dreams for me. Ignorant of how much I had been influenced by secular thinking, I was incredibly inconsistent in my Christian life.

I tell my own story because I believe my experience illustrates the problems many Christians face today. We have chosen a "lesser god" to worship, one bound by the limits of our own reason, by our modern skepticism, and by our desire to control our own lives. But even the most skeptical Christian can find a way out of this intellectual box and come to a more meaningful and satisfying understanding of spiritual life.

The Supernatural Denied

I and many of my fellow Christians have been guilty of the sin of syncretism, the blending of biblical faith with the secular environment. We have inherited this sin from the Enlightenment. Its roots begin with the Jewish philosopher Spinoza (born in 1634), the father of modern biblical criticism, who equated God's order with nature's order. For him the universe was determined by the laws of cause and effect and these laws were simply an extension of God himself.[2] According to this theory, to assert that God acts against the laws of nature is to assert that God acts against himself, an evident absurdity. That Spinoza automatically excluded miracles by this thesis is clear, and his assumption about God was to become one of the major canons of biblical studies. This form of reasoning found its way into my thinking and caused me a good deal of confusion. I didn't go so far as to deny miracles, but I did not expect that God would work outside of a cause and effect system and personally intervene in my life or in the life of anyone else.

This anti-supernatural worldview has come to dominate our perception of the Christian faith in the West. In *The Decline and Fall of the Roman Empire* (published in 1776), Edward Gibbon looks at the dynamic movement of Christianity as it invaded the Roman Empire. While recognizing that the early Christians expected supernatural events and experiences, Gibbon no longer lives in their world. He admits that "the Christian church, from the time of the apostles and their first disciples, has claimed an uninterrupted succession of miraculous powers, the gift of tongues, of vision, and of prophecy, the power of expelling demons, of healing the sick, and of raising the dead."[3] He goes on to suppose, like many of us today, that there must have been some period when miracles were "either suddenly or gradually withdrawn from the ... church."[4] More honest than many Christians, Gibbon now admits his bias: "In modern times, a latent and even involuntary skepticism adheres to the most pious dispositions. Their admission of supernatural truths is much less an active consent than a cold and passive acquiescence." Here we see that Gibbon's "modern times" has outlasted him by 200 years and that his "cold and passive acquiescence" toward supernatural truths describes much of our theological education and church-life today, however formally "evangelical" it may be.

This diagnosis creates a certain amount of anxiety for me personally because, as I have already noted, I was raised on the so-called modern scientific worldview. Since this was my perception of reality, I was never critical about the way in which I had been taught to approach life. My father, educated as an engineer at the Harvard of the '20s, taught me, "A place for everything and everything in its place." Following Newton's view of an orderly natural world, he told me that there was also an order to my world. My job was to discover it and fit everything into it.

My mother also contributed to my worldview. Believing in progress she taught me, "Leave the world a better place than you found it." Between my father and my mother, then, I was busy ordering the world and improving it. These two values set me up for frustration since it was impossible to do both with equal vigour at the same time.

Challenging these enduring myths of order and progress in Western civilization, Jesus Christ claimed me when I was fifteen years of age. While he changed my heart, I did not allow him to change my mind. In some respects, my conversion was an evangelical interruption that later became a source of major conflict and confusion. Since I was still busy trying to get everything into its place and, at the same time, trying to improve the world, I was naturally attracted to the Presbyterian church because of its attention to order and social concerns.

John Calvin's demanding legal mind created a consistent theology and a form of church government during the Protestant Reformation that became my home. In it, my theological education provided me with a system of doctrine with which to control my faith, exegetical tools with which to control the Bible, management tools with which to control the church, and counseling techniques with which to control people. I am not denying that there is order to life or that reason is a gift of God. What I am denying is our autonomy in the use of God's gifts. My autonomous approach began to change during the '60s. The ultimate consequence would be a serious personal crisis followed by a radical shift in my perception of reality.

The Counter-Culture Revolt

After being raised in the benevolent Eisenhower era, educated to be a pastor, and comfortable in my ministry to well-groomed sorority and fraternity students from the University of Southern California, I was unprepared for the hippies from the counter-culture who flooded Hollywood Boulevard near our church. Rebelling against what they called the "plastic" society and its institutions, and fearful of the undeclared Vietnam War, this drop-out generation immersed itself in drugs and acid rock, demanding "peace, love, and brotherhood." Our whole "technological society" was now under attack as the perceived enemy. Moreover, its rational basis in the Enlightenment was also challenged. As former Harvard Professor Timothy Leary put it, "Reason is a tissue-thin artifact easily destroyed by a slight alteration in the body's biochemistry [through hallucinogenic drugs]."[5] Suddenly, everything was up for grabs and all of this was about to become intensely personal for me.

While shaking hands at the church door on a warm, summer Sunday in the mid-60s, I noticed a young woman loitering. She was crying softly, the mascara running down her cheeks. After motioning for her to join me in a pew, we began to talk. Her background emerged quickly: thrown out by her mother several years before, she had drifted to the Sunset Strip in Hollywood where she had lived with a series of young men. Now unmarried and pregnant, she had visited the largest church she could find in order to lose herself in the crowd. The message that morning, however, had stopped her. In the next twenty minutes we talked over the basic gospel. At one point she protested that she was too sinful for God to love her, but soon it was all over. We prayed, and I had my first "hippie" convert on my hands.

This young woman was to take me onto the streets of Hollywood. Drug addicts, drag queens, and hosts of broken, abused lives lay ahead. We opened a coffee house called "The Salt Company" and crashpads and a job program soon followed. I, however, was torn between the cries of the street and the powerful establishment of the Presbyterian church. Trying to move the church into ministry began to break me. I could no longer control events. If there was a place for everything, as my father had taught me, I could not find it.

Things came to a head when I was up for two straight nights with a young man threatening suicide. Under severe emotional and physical strain, I noticed a curious thing: my heart began to skip every third beat. Moreover, a good night's sleep did not reverse the symptom. I recall teaching my large college class on Sunday mornings and watching the sweat drop onto my Bible as I held the podium to keep from fainting. Finally, I went to a doctor, a cross between Amos and Jeremiah, who ordered me out of town for a complete rest. I followed his orders obediently.

Now my whole life was in crisis, emotionally, physically, and spiritually. Hollywood was not a middle-class community with neatly manicured lawns and well-washed children. Instead, it was a large, dirty, broken city where I was taking drug addicts to de-tox centers and hosting dozens of street people for dinner. The crisis, as I have noted, threatened my worldview. The absolute power of reason and its control crumbled. This was not Enlightenment order; this was post-Enlightenment chaos.

On the streets of Hollywood I fought a sea of drugs, violence, and sexual brokenness. There I found moral anarchy, insanity, and suicide. A graffiti on the wall of a French cafe at the end of World War II summed up the nihilism which I experienced: "Don't kill time, kill yourself."

Through this seeming chaos God was chipping away at me. I was beginning to receive his cure as the anomaly of the counter-culture was breaking up my scientific worldview. Simply leading people to Jesus and getting them into church and Christian disciplines were not enough. How was I to deal with the wounds of the past and the addictions of the present? Was it possible that the devil was a real enemy after all? Could there be a power from God to deliver and transform life at its core? While my perceptions of reality were cracking, they were not easily abandoned. What would take their place? What would give me security and power in ministry?

Carl Becker in a series of lectures given at Yale University in 1932, described the framework for my experiences on the streets of Hollywood in 1968. He observes, "It has taken eight centuries to replace the conception of existence as divinely composed and purposeful drama by the conception of existence as a blindly running flux of disintegrating energy. But there are signs that the substitution is now fully accomplished. . . ." Becker then stated poignantly, "Man is but a foundling in the cosmos, abandoned by the forces that created him. Unparented, unassisted and undirected by omniscient or benevolent authority, he must fend for himself, and with the aid of his own limited intelligence find his way about in an indifferent universe."[6] As for my own confidence in reason and nature, it was now gone.

When the Vietnam War ended, I was able to postpone my questions and return to the quiet of college teaching. Here in the bosom of a fine, liberal arts campus, I could reassemble my vision of an orderly universe and let the dust settle. But the Claremont Colleges were to be no safe refuge.

Encountering the Power of God

What had been a personal and philosophical crisis for me in the '60s was to become a spiritual crisis in the '70s. At

Claremont I supposed that my classes in biblical studies would be both my strong card and my safety zone. I was, however, sadly mistaken. The issues of the '60s could not be put to rest, as, much to my discomfiture, I came upon a small book written by a former classmate, Walter Wink, who was at Union Seminary in New York. In *The Bible and Human Transformation* Wink applies the counter culture's critique of our rational, scientifically oriented society to the modern approach to the Bible, the very subject which I was teaching. Let me summarize his main points.

First of all, Wink shows that the scientific, historical method makes a false claim for objectivity. Assuming that it alone is free from human prejudice and cultural limitations, it cannot be self-critical. While it pretends to be value-neutral, such an ahistorical point of view is impossible to achieve. Even the scientist is determined by his own human frailties and his place in space and time. Moreover, because the scientific method limits itself to reason alone, it is blind to the irrational and unconscious in our lives. It systematically represses this error, however, by treating all reality as equivalent to the intellect. Wink concludes that scientific objectivism "pretends to be neutral when in fact the scholar, like everyone else, has racial, sexual, and class interests to which he is largely blind."[7]

Everything I had experienced on the streets of Hollywood prepared me for these barbs against my rationalistic faith. Was my teaching of religion, and more specifically the Bible, simply a veiled extension of an outdated and outmoded worldview which no longer worked? It suddenly dawned upon me that summer as I taught a class in "New Testament Introduction" at Fuller Seminary that I was really training future pastors to be scientists. The clear spiritual power witnessed to in the very texts we were studying were for us only a distant echo. By applying the scientific method to biblical studies I was teaching my students to distance themselves from the Bible with this false claim for objectivity. Moreover, I was not being honest about the enterprise.

Therefore, in midstream, I shifted. Rather than abandon the study of historical and literary issues, however, I continued the program, but self-critically. I used Walter Wink's observations to distance myself and my students from our method of study so that we could see both the method and its results. In this way we became self-critical toward what we were about. Such endeavors, however, became less and less satisfying, but I had no alternatives.

At this point, in the mid-70s, a graduate student at Claremont came into my life. With his long beard and sandals, it was clear that he was a leftover "flower-child." In fact, after having been heavily involved in drugs, he had become a Christian in Spokane, Washington in the mid-60s. Now, working on his doctorate in English literature, he looked me up because I was a somewhat controversial evangelical in the religion department of a secular campus. As our friendship developed, Steve expressed his concern for me one day: "Don, you need the power of the Holy Spirit in your life." Immediately my early warning system went on alert. Years before, I had been pursued by some charismatics in Hollywood who took me to small gatherings where they laid hands on people and, I supposed, told them to pray "banana" backwards. Sensing that they wanted me as a trophy for their religious enthusiasm, I wrote them off as a part of the Hollywood fringe. Now here it was, back again.

My response to Steve was to blandly admit that all of us need more of the Holy Spirit, but he would not accept my dodge. Periodically he brought up the subject, and I listened tolerantly because I liked him and the way his mind worked. Then, one night, after he had dinner with my wife and me, I allowed him to approach the subject of the power of the Spirit again and even to read a few standard passages from the Book of Acts concerning the coming of the Holy Spirit on the day of Pentecost (Acts 2), the pouring out of the Spirit during the Samaritan mission (Acts 8), Cornelius's conversion by the Spirit (Acts 10), and Paul's imparting the Spirit to John the

Baptist's disciples in Ephesus (Acts 19). In each case the power of the Spirit was evident, manifesting itself in gifts such as prophecy and tongues. I listened docilely and then we said, "Good night."

The next morning I awakened and spent some private time in prayer and Bible reading. Then it happened. The first thing that I noticed was that my fingers and toes began to tingle. As these physical sensations increased, my pulse sped up and my breathing became shortened. I sensed something (or better, Someone) coming over me. I responded with both fear and excitement. What was going on? Was it last night's spaghetti sauce? Or was God trying to do something more in me? I knew as I sat before my roll-top desk that I had to make a decision. Either I could go with what was happening to me or I could shut it off. I recall praying, "Lord, if this is you, if you want to do something more in my life, then I give you permission to do it." The sensations now increased and I had a great urge to go somewhere to be alone and pray.

Across town was a spot in the Glendale hills near my childhood home where I had often retreated as a new Christian. I quickly drove there and carrying my Bible hiked up the fire-break. Seated now amongst sage and sticky monkey, I began to pray. An urge engulfed me to praise God. As I spoke out this urge, joy exploded within me. My love for Jesus was inflamed and poured from me in tears and laughter. The ecstasy (and that is what it was) increased until English with its grammatical structure could no longer adequately express my feelings. At this point, it was as if God gave me a tool for praise and I began to babble my joy in syllables incoherent to me. The language flowed and as I spoke deliriously I thought with my mind how foolish and stupid all of this was. I was so glad to be alone. Nevertheless, it was wonderful, liberating, releasing. For perhaps the first time I was really worshiping the Lord with "joy unspeakable" (1 Pt 1:8).

In these hours which seemed like minutes, I was anointed by the Holy Spirit. He came upon me and filled me like that fountain of living water that Jesus promised in John 7:38. The counter-culture had cracked my shell, and then in God's sovereign time the free grace of the Holy Spirit came to fill my deep emptiness.

Having been taught that we receive all of the Spirit's filling in conversion/baptism, I had until now held that a second experience of the Spirit was unbiblical. A second experience was not valid because it seemed to add something to the finished work and finality of Christ. However, my experience now simply did not fit my old theology. At the same time, rather than adding something to Christ, Christ added something to me, and the validity of this was assured in my heartfelt desire to love, worship, and serve Jesus all the more.

Whatever theological problems may arise from this account, what I must attest to here is that for me this experience was biblical (it flowed from the Acts texts Steve shared with me the night before) and it was real. It also changed major aspects of my Christian life and brought to relevance several New Testament passages on the power and gifts of the Spirit. Now these texts claimed me and my ministry to come. I later found out that my experience was historically "evangelical" (with the possible exception of tongues). For example, Jonathan Edwards, the leader of the Great Awakening in America prior to the Revolutionary War, recounts being overcome by the "pure and sweet grace and love" of Christ in a vision. He writes,

> The Person of Christ appeared ... with an excellency great enough to swallow up all thoughts and conceptions, which continued, as near as I can judge, about an hour; such as to keep me a greater part of the time in a flood of tears, and weeping aloud. I felt an ardency of soul to be, what I know not otherwise how to express, emptied and annihilated; to lie in the dust, and to be full of Christ alone; to love Him with a holy and pure love; to trust in Him; to live upon Him; to serve Him and to be perfectly sanctified and made pure, with a divine and heavenly purity.[8]

Likewise, Dwight L. Moody, the great nineteenth century evangelist, gives a similar witness as he writes,

> I began to cry as never before, for a greater blessing from God. The hunger increased; I really felt I did not want to live any longer. I kept crying all the time that God would fill me with His Spirit. Well, one day in the City of New York—oh! what a day, I cannot describe it, I seldom refer to it. It is almost too sacred an experience to name.... I can only say, God revealed Himself to me, and I had such an experience of His love that I had to ask Him to stay His hand.[9]

Similarly, Michael Cassidy, a graduate of Cambridge University and a modern Moody to the great continent of Africa writes,

> [Late one night] sleep would not come to me. Instead, quite out of the blue, the Spirit of praise came upon my soul. All seemed to be release. All seemed to be freedom. Hour after hour I praised my God in unrestrained and unrestrainable doxology and song. In words of men and angels I rejoiced. No fatigue visited me that night. All my senses were vibrantly alive to God. The Holy Spirit was blessing me. Wave upon wave, it seemed. Flow upon flow. He seemed to be bubbling up from within, surrounding from without, ascending from below and descending from above.... Somewhere in the early hours of the morning I said to myself, "I don't know the correct biblical name for this, but this is the experience I've heard others talk of."[10]

Thus, unknown to me then, I had been moved into the biblical and evangelical mainstream by the coming of the Spirit in power into my life.

An essential part of my encounter with the Holy Spirit and resulting experience was the further breaking up of my scientific bias. Suddenly, I had been catapulted over the laws of reason and nature into an experience of the living God which was congruent with Jesus' anointing by the Spirit at his baptism and the apostles' anointing by the Spirit at Pentecost. What I would do with this, or better, what this would do with me, remained unknown. But the reality was there and my experience forced this anomaly, the power of the Spirit, to become part of my worldview. I now had a deep, inner assurance of my salvation which, try as I might, I could not shake. Furthermore, I had a clear experience of giving up my control without going out of control (as I had feared). Instead, I had gone under the Spirit's control. Finally, my love for Jesus was rekindled, and I received a gift called "tongues" or "prayer language" with which to pray to him.

In their book *The Emerging Order,* Rifkin and Howard define the contemporary charismatic movement as a "monumental assault on the modern age itself." The gifts of faith healing, speaking in tongues, and prophecy challenge our secular culture to its core. Thus, they conclude, "These supernatural powers are beginning to replace science, technique, and reason as the critical reference points for interpreting one's day-to-day existence."[11] On my Glendale hillside I experienced this "monumental assault" directly. But why had it happened to me? I had few answers then. Although this event was so totally sovereign and gracious, it was also isolating. I had no immediate community with which to share it. That would have to wait until I was once again in the pastorate.

My wife Kathryn and I moved to the San Diego area in the fall of 1979 in order to help some friends found a retreat center. Locating ourselves in the seaside village of La Jolla, I was invited by the pastor of a small Presbyterian church to fill in for him by preaching that next summer. This I did and, much to my surprise, when he returned, he resigned and left me with the church. Even in those first summer months we experienced growth as I taught the Bible from a strong evangelical perspective. As offerings and attendance increased we started small groups which later became weekly "home fellowships," forming the base of the church. The atmosphere was comfortable and things went reasonably well until 1983 when I entered into a period of intense anguish. If the '60s had created a personal and philosophical crisis for me, and if the '70s had led to a spiritual crisis, the '80s now provided an emotional crisis which was to send me on a quest for the healing power of Jesus in my life.

The Healing Mercy of Jesus

As is true for many, the years take their toll. Pain, repressed and forgotten, remains inside of us and, like Mount Saint Helens, its eruption may be surprising and costly. For my wife Kathryn and me, the eruption came in the spring of '83 when our marriage became severely threatened.

That spring, a letter from one of our students at Fuller Seminary found me feeling raw and broken. In it Craig encouraged me to hear a local pastor, John Wimber, teach what was to become a famous and controversial class in the School of World Missions, MC 510, "Signs, Wonders, and Church Growth." The thesis of the course was that where the church is growing dramatically today (especially in the Third World), the presence of God is being manifested by the direct action of the Holy Spirit. This takes place through "power evangelism" which is signed by healings, deliverance from demons, and other miraculous works of God. What made Wimber's class unique, however, was his structuring the course so that the students not only studied the power of God but also experienced it in a laboratory setting at the end of his lectures. Believing that Jesus is the "Word/Worker," Wimber, following his example, set about to be the same *in the classroom!* This radical change in methodology forced hundreds of students into a worldview shift as they experienced God's power and provoked so much controversy among the theological faculty that the class was finally abandoned. Moreover, the course was so popular that this action had to be justified in a book, *Ministry and the Miraculous: A case study at Fuller*

Theological Seminary which was produced by a task force of twelve scholars at the seminary. While I was unable to attend any of Wimber's lectures, I finally did manage to drop in on his evening church service in May of 1983. It proved to be one of those life-changing moments for me.

I vividly recall entering the gymnasium of Canyon High School in Anaheim Hills, a bedroom community in the Southern California sprawl. On this warm spring night 2000 people were singing together. As I surveyed the scene, I saw a small band on a raised platform leading the music and hundreds of people giving themselves to simple, melodious "praise songs." Some had their eyes closed. Some lifted their hands in worship. Most were seated, although some stood. There was an unselfconscious air to the whole event; these worshipers were not focused on each other or on the band at the front. By the smiles on many faces and not a few tears, it was clear to me that their hearts were with the Lord. At the same time, there was no disorder as the musicians moved from one song to another and the congregation followed without hymnals or overhead projectors. Clearly, most knew the music and I found myself able to enter into the simplicity of it all. Then it struck me—we were all a choir before the Lord, filling the place with praise. My heaviness lifted. I felt the Spirit awaken my heart, as I, along with so many others, was drawn into the presence of the living God.

After forty minutes of worship, John Wimber turned his electric keyboard into a pulpit and went on to teach from Galatians. Expecting to hear some shallow message left over from the '60s "Jesus Movement" about the end of the world, I was amazed to receive straight forward teaching grounded in solid biblical theology. After this exposition, which made me feel theologically at home, Wimber gave several supernatural "words of knowledge" about those whom God wanted to heal, and then he led a time of "prayer ministry."

I walked out into the lengthening shadows of that California night refreshed and amazed. "Whatever worship is," I thought to myself, "this is it: state of the art." Moreover, John's teaching hooked me and his emphasis on God's healing power raised hope for my damaged heart. Returning the next Sunday evening, I took courage and introduced myself to him after the service. Much to my surprise, John was to become my pastor and teacher in the months that followed.

Because of my emotional pain, I had been brought to a longing for healing and an openness to being prayed for that I had never known. What I demanded was the assurance that such a healing ministry was on solid scriptural grounds. Moreover, I needed the role model of someone who was doing it with integrity. I found both of these requirements in Wimber, and I was especially impressed by the hundreds of people in his church praying for the sick after the service which made it a "body ministry" rather than a spectacle focused on one individual.

In the weeks that followed, Wimber took me with him. We drove together to a healing seminar which he taught at the First Baptist Church of Bakersfield. Being new to all this and inherently conservative (control was and is still an issue for me), I sat frozen in my chair and watched Wimber work. Others around me were stepping out to join the team of experienced leaders which he had brought with him. But I was still in my analytical stage. Therefore, the best part for me was Wimber's vulnerability and honesty. I recall asking him how he prepared for praying for the sick. Expecting him to reveal a deep spiritual secret, Wimber replied, "I drink a diet Coke." This was not flippant. Since he had an intimate relationship with Jesus and a dependence upon the Holy Spirit, Wimber moved easily in being fully human at the same time.

My experience on the hillside in Glendale had brought to life the New Testament texts about the power of the Spirit and his gifts for me. Now my emotional pain and Wimber's message and ministry led me to believe in the healing mercy of Jesus and its apostolic continuation for me as well. Here was another shift in my perception of reality. The biblical worldview was beginning to shape my thinking and behavior more and more.

The task before me now was to bring this back to our church in La Jolla. As I considered risking praying for the sick at home, I needed to clarify my own position. This led me to teach on the biblical basis for healing throughout that summer. Some in the congregation were excited. Others were nervous. Others left. As I taught and studied, my experience of the power of the Spirit began to make sense. God had empowered me for ministry and now the full extent of that ministry lay ahead. And what was it to be? Jesus' ministry in me, through me, and through the church, his body—nothing more and nothing less.

One of my closest friends at that time was Mark, a man who had had a spectacular conversion several years earlier. One night, I asked him to pray for my healing from past emotional pain. To prepare for this he fasted for a full day. When we met, he laid his hands upon me as he prayed. After some intercession, Mark continued in tongues and as he did, Jesus came to me in an inner vision, taking me back to a moment in my childhood which had been damaging to me and disruptive to my marriage. Now entering into that moment, God took the rejection and guilt which I had experienced. That night was a breakthrough for me. Later, I reflected on the fact that God is not timebound. My past is as accessible to his healing touch as my present.

What had begun that spring with Wimber at the Vineyard now was complete. Is Jesus' healing ministry for the church today? I can only say, with the man born blind, "Whereas I was blind, now I see" (Jn 9:25). As another divine intervention pushed out the perimeters of my experience, my theology and my functional worldview expanded once again.

What lay ahead for me and for my church were many struggles as we tried to implement Jesus' healing ministry in our midst. What happens to those who are offended by this? What about abuses? What about those who aren't healed? How can healing lower back pain be equated with the signs and wonders of Jesus' mighty ministry? Isn't our preoccupation with health narcissistic? What about the call to suffer? Aren't miracles simply for the Apostolic Age? In the chapters ahead I will respond to many of these questions. Our first task, however, which was mine also in 1983, is to lay the biblical foundation.

It is my thesis that we need both a proper diagnosis and a proper cure in order to reverse the secular subversion of the church. With autobiographical risk I have offered a diagnosis in this chapter. In those that follow I will propose a cure as we survey the whole of biblical revelation and see God's claim upon us. For the Bible, God is King and we are called into his kingdom where he wants to reign directly and dynamically in our lives and extend his reign through us to this hostile, fallen world. Only when we have been established in this biblical worldview both intellectually and experientially, will we be rid of our bias against miracles. In this way will we be prepared for God's direct actions to break in upon us, even if, at times, we wish they wouldn't.

TWO

The Reign of God

JESUS PROCLAIMED THE MESSAGE of the kingdom because he knew that God is King, but how can we believe this when, as the heirs of the Enlightenment, we assume that our fate is in our own hands rather than his? How can the message and ministry of Jesus penetrate the anti-supernaturalism of our culture and the chaos of our current history and our personal lives?

When I attended Princeton as an undergraduate in the mid-50s I had the illusion that I could understand the world as an ordered place. As we students made our way to the required chapel services, my classmates and I still nominally believed in the University's motto, "Under God we prosper." However, today we no longer see ourselves as "under God" or any other authority. Since relativism characterizes our age, we have abandoned the assumption that there is a coherent core of knowledge to be learned. Students merely pick their way to a degree from a smorgasboard of options. Robert Hutchins, the former President of the University of Chicago, defines the modern university as a series of separate schools and departments held together by a central heating system. And after reviewing the present chaos, Edward Fiske, Education Editor for *The New York Times*, concludes, ". . . the fundamental problem . . . remains that of finding a substitute for the religious ideals that undergirded [the universities]... through the mid-19th Century."[1]

If this is true for the microcosm of our institutions of higher education, it only reflects the macrocosm of our society. Whether we need a new worldview or need to recover a biblical worldview, the pressing question before us now is, "How have we come so far?" Allan Bloom, in his best-selling book, *The Closing of the American Mind,* provides us with some answers.

Bloom points out that the Enlightenment substituted nature for the divine authority of God as its supreme reality. Modern man, however, has abandoned both God and nature, ending up with only himself as a reference point—"to each his own." Cut free from any divine or rational order, all that remains is for us to swim alone in the soup of relativism, mouthing selfish slogans such as "If it feels good, do it" (even if the "it" is a shot of heroin with a dirty needle which will give us AIDS). Our highest value now is to be open to anything and everything. This has created, according to Bloom, the "democratic personality," which is just as receptive to a Marxist or a Hari Krishna as to Margaret Thatcher or the Pope.

Relativism, however, is an intellectual evil; to be absolutely open-minded is to be empty-minded. To look into the mind of a relativist, therefore, is to peer into nothingness. Once we embrace relativism, we have no standards by which to judge or evaluate anything, making us defenseless against error or evil. Rather than correcting mistakes in order to be right, the relativist's point is not to think that he is right at all. This results in nihilism where the external becomes formless and the internal becomes empty.

As a rock musician friend of mine once told me, "I looked deeply into myself and found that nothing was there" (he quickly became a Christian). Because of our isolation and accompanying relativism, Bloom asserts, "America is experienced not as a common project but as a framework within which people are only individuals, where they are left alone."[2]

Along with relativism we are also unequivocally committed

to equality. If our forefathers overthrew the British crown for the sake of political freedom, we have overthrown the natural order for the sake of personal freedom. Thus, even if nature differentiates between male and female and parents and children, such distinctions must be obliterated for the sake of this ideology.[3] Paternal authority is turned into parental authority. A father's divine or natural right to rule now becomes the parents' responsibility to care for their children for the sake of the children's freedom. As Bloom concludes, "There is nothing left of the reverence toward the father as the symbol of the divine on earth, the unquestioned bearer of authority."[4] This means that all authority is now suspect; no one is safe. What impact has this isolated, "democratic personality," cut free from all authority or structure, had upon the church?

The church, too, has shifted away from divine sovereignty to human responsibility, believing that our fate and God's fate lie in our hands. As one of our hallmark hymns puts it:

Rise up O men of God,
The church for you doth wait.
Her strength unequal to the task,
Rise up and make her great.

This sentiment has clearly guided the liberal church with its "social gospel," designed to "bring in the kingdom of God" by moral and social reform (and political action). It has also found its recent expression in "Liberation Theology," rooted in the Third World, which boldly advocates armed revolt on a Marxist model to support God's just identification with the poor. At the same time, this humanistic sentiment has also captured the evangelical and fundamentalist church. We can see this in the great 19th Century evangelist, Charles Finney, who having rejected the older Calvinism, taught "laws" of revival which, when obeyed with good old American "get-up-and-go," forced God's hand. Here is evidence for the clear shift from divine sovereignty to human responsibility with an accompanying technology of revival. Religion can now be manipulated and marketed by televangelists like soap. Madison Avenue research will guarantee a percentage response. This results in an evangelical environment where we suppose that we can enthrone God in our hearts, as if his authority and power come from his subjects, "we the people." By making freedom and "moral responsibility" our idols (a minor biblical theme after the Fall which only justifies God's judgment, see Romans 1), we reduce God to a divine bellboy anxiously waiting to carry our bags. Parallel to liberal theology, evangelical theology now has its advocates, on the extreme edges, working to fulfill the command given to us in Genesis 1:26 to have dominion over the earth. Their program is to establish God's government in the here and now, not by evangelism or by the return of Christ, but by instituting Old Testament legislation through political action.

Whether we are liberals bringing in the kingdom for a just society or conservatives enthroning Christ as King in our hearts and then going faithfully to the voting booth to ensure his reign, we all end up in charge, reflecting our common "democratic personality" rather than a biblical "theocratic personality." For us, Jesus' announcement of the kingdom of God must fall upon uncomprehending ears.

In order for this fog to lift, we must take a fresh look at the structure of the Bible. Many of us hesitate to do this because of the size of the task. To open the Bible is to enter a library of books. Others falter because they have no guidelines to take them through thousands of years of biblical history. They ask in dismay, "Where do we even begin?" Still others assume that our Sunday School education is enough. However, we are often wrong because, sadly, such teaching is fragmentary and many times based upon unbiblical assumptions or a very narrow concept of God. Our task then is to go to the Bible itself, to see the forest, and not get lost in the trees. The fact that God is King becomes the crucial key for our understanding the whole of Scripture from Genesis to Revelation, as we shall see.

Recovering a Biblical Worldview

Whenever God shows himself in his heavenly reign throughout the Bible, he is seen seated upon his throne, sovereign over all things. In order for us to recover an understanding of this we must journey back into a time when God clearly took hold of one nation, Israel, and revealed to her his absolute authority. Here we see what our secular eyes never imagined possible: a loving God, commanding nature and history with supernatural power, personally active in the lives of his people, establishing his law, and shaping the destiny of all mankind. He is not a mythological figure now outdated because we have progressed beyond a need for him. His reign cannot be voted in or out of history. In the Old Testament we learn that God's purposes are everlasting, even to our age. We can either fall humbly before him in submission to his will or rebel against him. He will bless us in our obedience or destroy us in our disobedience. Reality offers us no other alternatives.

Let us recapture this understanding of God as King. Whenever he reveals himself to Israel, God shows her his regal splendor. His people cannot see his face, but fall prostrate before him in fear and awe. In response, even the earth trembles and the heavens shake. As King, therefore, he assaults Egypt with signs and wonders delivering his people from Pharaoh's bondage. He sends the plagues, parts the sea, guides Israel with a cloud and pillar of fire, reveals his mind to Moses, and goes behind and before his people. They know who he is. As God sets up his court on Mount Sinai, he grants a vision of himself reigning in glory. Nature responds with "thunder and lightning flashes and a thick cloud" (Ex 19:16), and with "fire . . . smoke" and the whole mountain quakes violently (Ex 19:18). Here we learn, as the Israelites did, that it is an awesome thing for God to come down from heaven and make himself known to us. He is not to be trifled with, for he is the mighty King, he is Yahweh present in the midst of his people, and all we can do is surrender our lives to him.

After Israel settled the Promised Land, her prophets knew well the majesty of Yahweh. For instance, Isaiah saw the Lord "sitting on a throne, lofty and exalted, with the train of His robe filling the temple" (Is 6:1). Around him stand a host of great angelic beings called seraphim or "shining ones" who with a loud voice cry out, "Holy, holy, holy is the Lord of hosts, the whole earth is full of His glory" (Is 6:3). Like any man who is granted a glimpse of the King of the universe, Isaiah is properly staggered by this sight. God's holiness, his astounding glory, his utter transcendence over all creation cuts Isaiah to the heart. "Woe is me," he cries, "for I am ruined!" Why does Isaiah respond so? Had not God invited him to look freely upon the grandeur of God? But for Isaiah to see the Lord meant that he was able for the first time to see himself. He confronts his own sin, claiming that he is "a man of unclean lips," who also lives among people of unclean lips. "For my eyes have seen the King, the LORD of hosts" (Is 6:5). When we set our eyes upon the King, we are immediately broken and groveling. This vision of true glory and holiness divests us of all notions of our own power and knowledge and strips away our own presumptuous schemes to control our own lives. We would say with Isaiah:

For the LORD is our judge,
The LORD is our lawgiver,
The LORD is our king;
He will save us. (Is 33:22)

The revelation of God as King is also given to Ezekiel when he received his call to be a prophet. Removed from Jerusalem to Babylon, he recounts, "While I was by the river Chebar among the exiles, the heavens were opened and I saw visions of God" (Ez 1:1). These visions included a storm wind, "a great cloud with fire flashing forth continually" with "a bright light around it, and in its midst something like glowing metal in the midst of the fire" (Ez 1:4). Within this great cloud were four human-like, living beings with multiple faces and wings. An expanse like crystal extended over their heads and above that expanse "there was something resembling a throne . . . and on that . . , high up, was a figure with the appearance of a man" (Ez 1:26). The figure looked like glowing metal and fire, and there was a "radiance around Him" like a rainbow (Ez 1:27-28). Ezekiel then concludes, "Such was the appearance of the likeness of the glory of the LORD. And when I saw it, I fell on my face" (Ez 1:28). Like Isaiah, he is in the dust before God. Here his body language expresses his submission, and in this position he is now called to be a prophet.

Daniel too sees God seated upon a throne as "the Ancient of Days." The sight of the heavenly King with his court gathered before him is awesome:

His throne was ablaze with flames,
Its wheels were a burning fire.
A river of fire was flowing
And coming out from before Him;
Thousands upon thousands were attending Him,
And myriads upon myriads were standing before Him.
(Dn 7:9-10)

One "like a Son of Man" is then presented to the Ancient of Days and given "dominion, glory and a kingdom, that all the peoples, nations, and men of every language might serve Him. His dominion is an everlasting dominion which will not pass away." (Dn 7:13-14)

Here we see the sovereign rule of God now entrusted to this glorious Son of Man. With this vision of God as King, and the Son of Man executing his reign, then, we are moving toward the great fulfillment of God's sovereignty expressed in the coming of the Messiah.

It is no surprise that along with Old Testament law, history, and prophecy, the psalter also extols the reign of God. Psalm 10:16 announces: "The LORD is King forever and ever; nations have perished from His land." The psalmists also personally submit to the Lord, addressing him in prayer as "My King and my God" (Ps 5:2), and confessing, "Thou art my King, O God" (Ps 44:4). Furthermore, they view his reign as *universal*, he is "a great King over all the earth" (Ps 47:2, see verses 7-8), and *absolute,* He is "a great King above all gods" (Ps 95:3).

These are but a few examples from Scripture which offer evidence that God is King, that this belief is consistent and pervasive throughout Israel's history, determining her thought and piety. As we have seen, he is seated in majesty with a sea of angels gathered before him, commanding the kingdoms of this earth and judging his people. Moreover, it is God who delegates his reign to the Son of Man and executes it through him. For the Bible, God is King from beginning to end.

Our Response

This now gives us the proper framework for understanding what the Jews heard when Jesus came into Galilee proclaiming that the kingdom of God is "at hand" (Mk 1:15). Immediately they knew that he was heralding the inbreaking of that messianic and apocalyptic rule which the prophets had promised and for which their hearts longed. Expectations ran high that God would bare his arm and break Satan's evil domain manifested in the totalitarian oppression of Rome. With her enemies expelled, Israel would again prosper under the direct authority and reign of God. Through his messianic King a time of unparalleled peace and prosperity would be Israel's and her gift to the Gentile nations as they came to Mount Zion. To be under God's direct, sovereign rule is to find true freedom, freedom from Satan, sin and death. No wonder Jesus' proclamation of God's kingdom sent an electric shock throughout Israel. They had longed for the King to come.

Do we, who have received God's revelation as expressed in Scripture and in the coming of the Messiah, long for God to rule over us and restore us in the power of his Spirit? Or do many of us find signs, wonders, prophetic visions, and men prostrate in the dust before God a bit too otherworldly for our sensibilities? I would venture to say that most of us know little about how to respond to the reign of God today.

It is my firm conviction that as we recapture the vision of God's kingdom and worship him, we will experience his power as it comes mightily upon us. We will be recalled from our theological drift and receive secure moorings for a new integration of our thought and life. I have seen the kingdom come in the power of signs and wonders. God is now present among his people and ready to make himself known to us as we confess him as Lord. Let us enter into the experience of his majesty which has always been a hallmark of revival in the history of the church.

John Wesley records just such a profound revival experience in his Journal for January 1, 1739, seven months after his conversion:

> Hall, Hinching, Ingham, Whitefield, Hutching and my brother Charles were present at our love feast in Fetter Lane with about sixty of our brethren. About three in the morning as we were continuing constant in prayer the power of God came mightily upon us, insomuch that many cried out for exulting joy and many fell to the ground. As soon as we were recovered a little from the awe and amazement at the presence of His Majesty, we broke out with one voice, "We praise Thee O God, we acknowledge Thee to be the Lord."[5]

THREE

Recovering the Christian Mind

HARRY BLAMIRES HAS OBSERVED that as a consequence of the Enlightenment there is no longer a "Christian mind." That is, there is no agreed basis upon which to communicate "Christianly." He writes, "Except over a very narrow field of thinking, chiefly touching questions of strictly personal conduct, we Christians in the modern world accept, for the purpose of mental activity, a frame of reference constructed by the secular mind and a set of criteria reflecting secular evaluations."[1] This absence of a set of common assumptions which will allow Christians to talk clearly with each other manifests itself in our contradictory approaches to the Bible. Consider, for example, our various interpretations of the miraculous events which we find there or our struggle with God's wrath or our tortured explanations of Israel's "holy wars." Allan Bloom notes that the Bible created our common culture "as the ... model for a vision of the order of the whole of things ..." He concludes that now "the very idea of such a total book and the possibility and necessity of a world-explanation is disappearing..." This loss of the Bible as a "total book" has monumental implications. "Contrary to what is commonly thought, without the book even the idea of the order of the whole is lost."² We must now ask ourselves candidly, do we view the Bible as this "total book?" Most of us at best have a few favorite stories such as Noah and the ark and David and Goliath which seem loosely held together by a series of inspirational verses. When pushed we even have a hard time narrating the events of Jesus' life with any meaningful continuity. No wonder our Christian mind looks like a Picasso painting, disjointed and fragmented behind splashes of color. What, then, must we do?

The recovery of the Christian mind and a comprehensive sense of reality will only take place when we grasp once again the key biblical theme which, as we have proposed in the last chapter, is centered in the fact that God is King. But what is the content of this confession? Turn with me to the world within which Israel came into being as a people.

King Hammurabi: An Example of the Ideal Ruler

In the summer of 1958, as my college graduation present, I traveled in Europe and the Middle East. There I saw first hand the ancestral graveyard of our civilization: the forum in Rome, the Parthenon in Athens, the walls of Nineveh. Especially impressive were the anchor points of the Fertile Crescent, the vast remains of Egyptian culture in the west and the excavations of Ur of the Chaldees, south of Babylon, in the east. It was in this context that God made himself known to Israel and called her into being as his people.

Genesis, the opening book of the Bible, must be understood within the setting of Sumerian civilization. Coming from Ur, one of its major cities (Gn 11:31), Abraham inherited a highly developed sense of divine kingship from this culture. A migrant people, the Sumerians arrived in Mesopotamia in the latter half of the fourth millennium B.C. Here they superimposed one of the first urban civilizations upon peasant farmers.³ This resulted in the unification of small communities under a central government, commanding large economic resources and manpower. The Sumerian worldview was dynamic, with a pantheon of gods whose exploits described chaos and its conquest. Centralized rule was seen as their gift, making life possible.

Although each city had its own tutelary deity, Enlil, the air god who ruled Nippur, headed the divine hierarchy. His decisions, however, were made in consultation with a heavenly council which reflected the structure of human kingship as well. Thus, the ancient states were built around the temple of a tribal deity which was ruled by a priest-king. Local rulers, mediators between heaven and earth, were called to serve the gods and do their will. Each city was the property of its god, then, and its citizens were its slaves. The important point here is that Abraham responded to God's call in the context of a theocratic culture through which he would now understand that Yahweh is King.

At the other end of the Fertile Crescent lay Egypt where, one day, Israel would languish in slavery. The pyramids, the temples at Luxor, housing huge representations of the Pharaohs such as Rameses II, and the cavernous tombs in the Valley of the Kings all bear witness to a great civilization now dust. Like Mesopotamia, Egypt also had an integrated religious worldview. Rather than the king being God's representative, however, Pharaoh was god-incarnate, sovereign over all. In Egypt Israel both understood and suffered under a fully developed and rationalized theology of divine kingship.

Israel's roots, however, lay in Mesopotamia. In order to understand the idea of kingship for Israel in this context, we now turn to the specific example of one of the best-known Babylonian rulers.

Hammurabi, immortalized by the Code of Hammurabi, a stone pillar containing the laws of his empire, ruled Babylon from 1728-1686 B.C. He stands as the ideal model of kingship in ancient theocratic culture. His example provides for us a framework for understanding Yahweh, the perfect King. As king of Babylon, Hammurabi was responsible for maintaining proper *worship*. He ruled by divine right, being called by the gods to his throne through Marduk, the god of Babylon. As a result, he exercised the gods' authority on earth and devoted his life to them by, among other things, building and maintaining their temples. In the epilogue to his code, Hammurabi confessed: "The great gods called me, so I became the beneficient shepherd whose scepter is righteous; my benign shadow is spread over my city."[4] Like England's kings and queens, he was the head of the church and the defender of the faith, ruling a theocratic society.

Hammurabi was responsible for establishing *justice* for his subjects and for fostering their *material prosperity*. After confessing his piety, like a good politician, he stated the purpose of his reign: it is to promote the welfare of the people. To do this he was to cause justice to prevail in the land, to destroy the wicked and the evil, in order that the strong might not oppress the weak. He was a Moses who makes law prevail; who guides the people aright. Like Solomon he was the wise one, the administrator; the one who plumbed the depths of wisdom. He established the welfare of the people through establishing and executing justice, it also comes through securing prosperity. Hammurabi, then, was the one who makes affluence and plenty abound through his public works. In the epilogue to the code he summarized his program: "I sought out peaceful regions for them; I overcame grievous difficulties; I caused light to rise on them."[5] Here the king not only ordered the land with justice, he also provided it with material blessing.

Hammurabi, as commander in chief, brought military and political *security* to his empire. He was a warrior like Joshua who strides through the four quarters of the world and makes the name of Babylon great. He was the one who seizes the foe. He was the chief of kings, "a fighter without peer." By his exploits in battle, Hammurabi was the savior of his people from distress, who establishes in security their portion in the midst of Babylon. Therefore, the epilogue declares: "I rooted out the enemy above and below; I made an end to war; I promoted the welfare of the land."[6] From Babylon, Hammurabi ruled a worldwide empire and brought it peace.

Finally, Hammurabi was the ideal ruler. He was the "devout, god-fearing prince," "the pious," "the wise king," "the solicitous, the perfect one," "the illustrious prince," "the warrior." Moreover, as king he acted as "the shepherd," "the monarch of kings," "god among kings," "the first of kings," "lord, adorned with scepter and crown," "the savior," "the ancient seed of royalty," "the sun of Babylon."[7] Called by the gods to his throne, Hammurabi's gifts to Babylon were worship, justice, prosperity, and security. The Scandinavian scholar Sigmund Mowinckel comments on these themes as he paints a comprehensive picture of kingship which Israel inherited from her Eastern environment:

> If we would sum up in one word what the people expected of the king who had been chosen and endowed with power, we may use the Mesopotamian's own expression and call him "the shepherd." Hammurabi, for example, so describes himself. But we may also sum it up in the Hebrew expression "the savior of his people." The king will "work salvation."... It means not only deliverance from earthly, cosmic, and demonic enemies, and from distress and misfortune, but good conditions, well-being, outward and inward prosperity, fertility in field, flock and nation, quietness and order in the state, "peace," and the like.[8]

Being merely human, Hammurabi passed into history. Later, his stone pillar was discovered by French archaeologists in the Elamite capital of Susa. Through his reign, however, we can understand the background for the biblical revelation that Yahweh is King. In a far greater way than Hammurabi could ever have imagined, he provides worship, justice, prosperity and security for his people. To this we now turn.

Yahweh, the Divine King

Unlike Hammurabi, who ruled by divine right, Yahweh rules because he is divine. That is, he rules by his *own* right. He is the one, true, living God. Beside him there is no other. It is interesting to note that never is he pictured in the Bible with a crown on his head. A crown symbolizes the glory and authority which has been delegated by a higher power. But God, in himself, possesses this glory and authority.

God does not wear a crown because he is a spirit and no physical representation can capture him. This separates him from the dumb idols who neither speak nor act, and, as he says to Moses, because of his glory, no one can see his face and live (Ex 33:20). Unlike earthly kings who filled their temples with statues of the gods, then, the Lord keeps the holy of holies in his temple empty, except for the Ark of the Covenant with its vacant mercy seat, and the Shekinah, the glory of his presence which comes and goes (see 1 Kings 8:10-11 and Ezekiel 10:18-19). This confirms that God is an invisible spirit who is transcendent and rules over all.

God's glory is boldly represented by his vestments. In Psalm 104:1-2 he is "clothed with splendor and majesty," covering himself "with light as with a cloak" (compare Psalm 93:1), and in Daniel his vesture is like white snow (Dn 7:9). At the same time, he can also be pictured in darkness: "Clouds and thick darkness surround Him" (Ps 97:2). Thus, he appears with a dense cloud and smoke on Mount Sinai (Ex 19:16-18). Both light and darkness, then, display different aspects of God's attributes: he is the One who is revealed and hidden. Neither nature nor reason are adequate ladders by which a fallen humanity can climb into his presence. Because of this, most of our pictures of him are woefully inadequate. God is greater than a philosophical "first cause" or a pop singer's "man upstairs." His glory is beyond our comprehension and we can know him only as he chooses to make himself known.

Garbed in light, enveloped in darkness, God exercises kingly rule from his throne. As the psalmists confess: "God sits on His holy throne" (Ps 47:8); "The LORD's throne is in heaven" (Ps 11:4, see Psalm 103:19; Isaiah 66:1); "Thy throne, O God, is forever and ever" (Ps 45:6, see Psalm 93:2). The descriptions of God's throne stretch the limits of our language. It is like lapis lazuli, a deep blue gem (Ez 1:26), or like sapphire (Ez 10:1), "ablaze with flames" and its wheels are "a burning fire" (Dn 7:9). A footstool is also attached: "Exalt the LORD our God, And worship at His footstool; Holy is He" (Ps 99:5, see Psalm 132:7). Furthermore, a river of fire flows from the throne (Dn 7:10, compare Psalm 97:3), and from the throne comes "flashes of lightning ... and peals of thunder" (Rv 4:5). Moreover, after the final battle with evil is won, it gushes with lifegiving water (Rv 22:1), while a rainbow surrounds it with radiance (Ez 1:28, compare Revelation 4:3). No wonder Isaiah cries out, "Woe is me," and Ezekiel falls on his face before the divine Majesty enthroned in such glory.

In light of the prophets' experiences, the fact that so many people today are bored or maintain only a mild interest during an average church service suggests more of God's absence than his presence.

Next, since Yahweh is King he must have a palace. His dwelling place is spoken of as heaven itself. Thus, the psalmist confesses, "The LORD is in His holy temple, the LORD's throne is in heaven" (Ps 11:4, see 1 Kings 8:30). At the same time, he transcends even his heavenly dwelling. As Solomon asks when he dedicates the temple in Jerusalem, "But will God indeed dwell on the earth?," and then replies, "Behold, heaven and the highest heaven cannot contain Thee, how much less this house which I have built!" (1 Kgs 8:27).

Moreover, God is surrounded by his heavenly court. He rules over hosts of angels who serve as counselors and messengers and are allotted authority over the nations of the earth. They also constitute his divine army. One of his most frequently repeated titles in the Old Testament is "The Lord [Yahweh] of hosts" or "The Lord, God of hosts."[9]

These angelic entities serve in a variety of capacities. Some function as guardians of God's throne. When the Ark of the Covenant, the portable box representing God's presence, is constructed by Israel in the wilderness, he commands that two golden cherubim be placed at opposite ends of his throne (symbolized by the mercy seat), covering it with their wings (Ex 25:18-20). Along with the cherubim, there are special angels who, like the ministers of earthly kings, fulfill a hierarchy of functions and offices before the Lord. For example, there is "the angel of the Lord" who appears often, from the patriarchal narratives to the monarchy. This angel delivers divine messages and mediates the divine presence, such as that granted to Moses in the burning bush (Ex 3:2). He also goes before Israel in the wilderness to protect her (Ex 14:19), and later executes God's judgment upon her rebellion (2 Sm 24:16). Other spirits also present themselves before the Lord and his court for special missions such as the deceiving spirit sent to entice King Ahab (1 Kgs 22:19-22).

In the latter period of Israel's history angelic identities become more concrete, especially in apocalyptic thought. For example, there is Gabriel who interprets Daniel's visions (Dn 8:16; 9:21) and who, because he "stands in the presence of God," brings the promises of John the Baptist's and Jesus' birth (Lk 1:19, 26-28). Also there is Michael, the "great prince," who guards Israel (Dn 12:1) and who is later identified as disputing with the devil for the body of Moses (Jude 9). He also leads God's angelic armies in heaven (Rv 12:7). Then, of course, there is Satan himself, the accuser of the brethren (Rv 12:10).

In our simple piety today, we reduce angels to the function of looking out for us like an electronic security device. These "guardian angels," we imagine, sit on the fenders of our cars as we drive. While I do not doubt that God sends angels for our protection, where is his flaming army engaging in battle on our behalf? Where are the divine messengers from the throne singing, "Glory to God in the highest!"? Not only are we prone to choose a "lesser god," but we often reduce the hosts of heaven to nothing more than our personal bodyguards.

Along with the angelic hosts, nature also serves God. As Psalm 104:4 tells us, "He makes the winds His messengers, flaming fire His ministers." Therefore, "Fire goes before Him, and burns up His adversaries round about" (Ps 97:3). In light of this we must ask, when was the last time that we saw a natural disaster as a supernatural disaster, coming from the throne of God? While pious England saw the Spanish Armada destroyed by a divine storm (a "Protestant wind"), we would attribute such an event to luck or chance. Again, this is another index of how secularized our worldview has become through the culture which presses in upon us.

Beyond God's court is his kingdom which includes both his reign and his realm. Like earthly kings, Yahweh has his subjects and his lands. Thus, his reign extends over all of creation in general (including Satan and his demons), and Israel and the redeemed Gentiles in particular. His realm includes all of creation in general, both heaven and earth, as we have seen, and the land of Israel in particular.

Worship

What is the purpose of Yahweh seated upon his throne, dwelling in his heavenly palace with his angelic court and his earthly subjects gathered before him? The answer can be given in a word: worship. While most Christians would agree with this, at the same time, we are confused as to what worship is. For example, the average person does not go to church in order to *give* himself to God in corporate worship, but in order to *get* something out of the service. Thus, we have trained a generation of believers to ask, "What's in it for me?" A successful, evangelical church, according to a well-known pastor, is one in which people's needs are met in the atmosphere of a "religious supermarket." It is no surprise, then, that we select a church building loaded with aesthetics and sit in the pew waiting to be inspired or even entertained. We end up judging the events of Sunday morning by whether our favorite hymns are sung, whether the choir is on key, whether the preacher is "relevant" (and brief), and whether people are friendly and remember our names. In other words, we view worship as designed to reinforce our basic selfishness, masked under "meeting our needs."

It is my experience that where the sense of God as King is being recovered in the church today, there is a corresponding renewal in worship as we *give* ourselves to him. Such worship centers not in praise given indirectly to God, as in the older hymns and gospel songs, but in praise given directly to God, as in the newer worship songs. At times it comes from an overpowering sense of his presence in the midst of his people and includes expressions of awe before his majesty and tenderness in response to his intimacy with us. With both order and ardor, it grows in intensity through sustained praise. Moreover, rather than the production of a professional few, it is the "sacrifice" of the whole people of God before his throne. The drama is not at the front of the sanctuary, with choir and clergy, but in the hearts of all the believers. When our praises ascend, God descends and dwells in the midst of his people. By his grace he then begins to work in remarkable ways. For example, I have personally seen people converted, filled with the Holy Spirit, and healed during such worship before the preaching ever begins.

For the Bible, the goal of all creation is to bow before the true and living God. As Psalm 103:19-22 expresses it:

The LORD has established His throne in the heavens;
And His sovereignty rules over all.
Bless the LORD, you His angels,
Mighty in strength, who perform His word,
Obeying the voice of His word!
Bless the LORD, all you His hosts,
You who serve Him, doing His will.

Bless the LORD, all you works of His,
In all places of His dominion;
Bless the LORD, O my soul!

Having examined the context of God's reign in heavenly splendor, we are now ready to ask: Who is this God whom we are to worship?

Our Creator and Sustainer

In her book, *The Lives of the Kings and Queens of England,* the editor, Antonia Fraser, writes, "It will be obvious to all but the most dedicated supporters of the Marxist theory of history that the personalities and peculiar characteristics of various sovereigns played at least some part in the shaping of events."[10] If this is true for British history, it is supremely true for biblical history. In fact, biblical history is authored and molded by the personality and the "peculiar characteristics" of Yahweh, "God of hosts." The content of his reign is determined by who he is as Creator, Judge, and Redeemer. We turn, then, to these themes.

As we have seen, Yahweh is eternally seated upon his throne and his court is always in session. From his throne he speaks creation into existence: "By the word of the LORD the heavens were made, and by the breath of His mouth all their host.... For He spoke, and it was done; He commanded, and it stood fast" (Ps 33:6, 9).[11] Moreover, the Creator is revealed through his creation: the heavens tell of his glory and the earth shows his handiwork (Ps 19:1, see Romans 1:18ff). Like an artist, he signs his work, and it is "good" (Gn 1:4ff). At the same time, God as Creator is distinct from that which he creates. He cannot be mystically merged with nature, as in many forms of Eastern religion and the "New Age" cults. Neither do we walk around with a little spark of divinity in us just waiting to be released. God is God. He is the Creator. We are the creation. And that is that.

Moreover, from his throne, God also *upholds* his creation:

"For the LORD is a great God, and a great King above all gods, in whose hand are the depths of the earth; the peaks of the mountains are His also" (Ps 95:3-4). Likewise, God, not gravity, provides for its stability: "The LORD reigns, He is clothed with majesty; The LORD has clothed and girded Himself with strength; Indeed, the world is firmly established, it will not be moved" (Ps 93:1, see Psalm 104:5). God is no absentee landlord, receiving revenues from us by monthly checks in the mail. He is on the property, supervising all that is being done there.

Furthermore, God, rather than Mother Nature, makes affluence and plenty abound. Thus, he sends the springs in the valleys (Ps 104:10), and "causes the grass to grow for the cattle" (Ps 104:14). Narrowing down God's care even further, Jesus tells us that he is also intimately involved in the smallest aspects of life on this planet; he sees the sparrow fall and numbers the hairs on our head (Mt 10:29-30). In the well-known words of the great Victorian preacher Charles Spurgeon, "He oversees all and overlooks none." By his providence God orders and upholds the world which he has created.

Along with the Lord's providential care, he also employs nature directly and dramatically for his purposes by pouring down fire upon a sinful city and splitting the sea for his people to pass through. At these points nature becomes a vehicle not for his faithfulness in predictable order but for his wrath and grace in signs and wonders. The God revealed here is wholly distinct from the "passive paternalism" of modern constitutional monarchies. Yahweh is more like an oriental despot whose word goes forth to accomplish his will, establishing his reign and overpowering all his enemies (see Isaiah 55:11).

Our Righteous Judge

Along with being the Creator, God is Judge. From his throne, he legislates and upholds the moral order which is the expression of his holiness. As the psalmist says, ". . . the strength of the King loves justice; Thou hast established equity; Thou hast executed justice and righteousness in Jacob" (Ps 99:4). While the ancient King Hammurabi received the law, Yahweh *is* the law. There is no sanction for ethics apart from him. There is no appeal beyond him. But what is the content of this judicial power?

First of all, God is righteous in his judgments, taking no bribes and making no errors. He judges by his own absolute character rather than by some external standard as kings like Hammurabi did, relying on the laws given to them. Therefore, as David confesses, "Thou art justified when Thou dost speak, And blameless when Thou dost judge" (Ps 51:4). Secondly, because of God's covenant relationship with Israel, she is the primary object of his judgments. Thus,

> He summons the heavens above,
> And the earth, to judge His people:
> "Gather My godly ones to Me,
> Those who have made a covenant with Me by sacrifice."
> And the heavens declare His righteousness,
> For God Himself is judge. (Ps 50:4-6)

Thirdly, along with Israel, the nations are also judged. Since God is righteous, he grants moral stability to the world which makes life possible here: "Let the nations be glad and sing for joy; For Thou wilt judge the peoples with uprightness, And guide the nations on the earth" (Ps 67:4).

Finally, the execution of God's judgments against evil is both present and future. In the present he reveals his "passive wrath" by allowing sinners to reap what they sow: "The LORD has made Himself known; He has executed judgment. In the work of his own hands the wicked is snared" (Ps 9:16; compare Romans 1:18ff). At the same time, the psalmists call again and again for God's "active wrath," his direct intervention: "Rise up, O Judge of the earth; Render recompense to the proud.

How long shall the wicked, O LORD, How long shall the wicked exult?" (Ps 94:2-3, see Psalm 7:6; 9:19; 82:8). Thus, God decimates Egypt and later tears down Jerusalem's walls. This "active wrath" will be consummated when he ushers in the final judgment: "For He is coming to judge the earth. He will judge the world in righteousness, And the peoples in His faithfulness" (Ps 96:13). As Judge, then, God combines the legislative, judicial, and executive branches of government within himself. He makes the law, judges by the law, and punishes lawbreakers. Recapturing an understanding of this righteousness of God will help us comprehend how he could will the brutal crucifixion of his Son at the hands of sinners in order to save us.

What we have seen so far is that God creates the world, sustains the world, and establishes and executes his moral order over it. There is one further attribute of God as King, however, which determines divine revelation and molds biblical history: he is full of grace and mercy because he is also the Redeemer.

Our Redeemer

In the Old Testament there is no direct identification made between God as Redeemer and his reigning upon his throne. There are at least two reasons for this. First of all, God's saving work is best expressed by verbs rather than by nouns. Since salvation is seen in his actions, he must arise from his throne and bare his arm in order to redeem us. He now becomes our Warrior-King, "a fighter without peer," who goes into battle on our behalf. Second, salvation in its institutional sense is related more to the altar than to the throne. Worship includes both God's demand and God's grace. As the priests offer blood-sacrifices, divine justice is satisfied and divine mercy revealed. It is God who intervenes in order to save us from our foes and who provides atonement for our sins. Let us now look at the specific content of God's work as Redeemer.

To begin with, God's people are redeemed. As the Lord says to Israel: "I will bring you out from under the burdens of the Egyptians, and I will deliver you from their bondage. I will also redeem you with an outstretched arm and with great judgments" (Ex 6:6, compare Mark 10:45). The motive behind this is his unconditional love. Thus, Moses asserts, ". . . because the LORD loved you . . . the LORD brought you out . . . and redeemed you . . ." (Dt 7:8). Why, however, do we need redemption? The general answer is because this is a fallen planet which holds us captive. Israel experienced this in Egypt as Yahweh redeemed her from the "house of slavery" (Dt 7:8; 13:5). Beyond idolatrous and political bondage, however, she needs to be redeemed from "troubles" (Ps 25:22), "iniquities" (Ps 130:8), and the power of Sheol or death (Ps 49:15, see Hosea 13:14). All of this climaxes in the New Testament when Jesus Christ redeemed us from our sins (Col 1:14), the "domain of darkness" (Col 1:13), the evil powers behind Jewish legalism (Gal 4:3, 9), and the "curse of the law" (Gal 3:13; 4:3, 9).

What, however, is the price of redemption? Normally in the ancient world redemption from slavery required the payment of a purchase price or ransom (see Psalm 49:7-8). In the Old Testament we see how God devises a plan to ransom his people through his Servant whom he has chosen (Is 49:7) by offering him as the sacrifice for sin (Is 53). Thus, God promises: "'And a Redeemer will come to Zion, And to those who turn from transgression in Jacob,' declares the Lord" (Is 59:20). The above texts clearly point us to the New Testament where Jesus, as the Messiah, redeems us through the blood of his cross (Eph 1:7).

These peculiar characteristics of Yahweh shape biblical history. He is the Creator who upholds his creation. He is the righteous Judge who executes his judgments. He is the Redeemer who himself pays the price of redemption. From creation to consummation the Bible consistently reveals God's character to us.

A Coherent Worldview

Illumined by the concept of kingship in the ancient Near East—the ideal king inspires worship and provides justice, prosperity, and security—what we have seen in this chapter is Yahweh as the perfect model of kingship. While he dwells in heaven, he supervises the affairs of earth and, at times, intervenes directly in them. As King he bears rule in his realm over his subjects which include both Israel and the nations. Therefore, he establishes the proper worship of himself. Moreover, he gives his law in order to create a just society and by his judgments he upholds that law. Commanding nature, he also offers prosperity to his people. Commanding history, he also makes them secure against their enemies. When they sin, however, he comes to save them. Rather than the "passive paternalism" of a constitutional monarchy, God determines our destiny.

We now see that it is impossible to understand the Bible apart from a worldview of consistent supernaturalism. To speak of God as the Lord of nature and history and to see him on his throne executing judgment and accomplishing redemption and, at the same time, to deny the reality of his sovereign, direct intervention with signs and wonders makes the assertions about his lordship empty ("mythological"), or, even worse, irrelevant.

Let me give you a contemporary example of how important this supernatural worldview is, especially when Christianity is presented to a world in need of God's direct intervention. Charles Kraft, a former missionary and now a professor at Fuller Theological Seminary writes that he was well prepared for overseas service in Nigeria except "in the area the Nigerians considered the most important—their relationships with the spirit world. These spirits, they told me, cause disease, accidents, and death, hinder fertility of people, animals and fields, bring drought, destroy relationships, harass the innocent and the like. . . ." Rather than bringing God's kingdom power against these evil forces and expelling them, the missionaries offered "Western medical techniques." However, Kraft adds, "[The natives] soon learned that our medicine can't handle many of their needs." What happened was that "we simply reproduced the secularized approach to illness and accident we had learned at home. We acted as though Western medicine was more effective than prayer. . . ." Exposed to doctors who were not Christians, the local people "discovered that whatever power was available in our clinics was inherent in the medicine, not in the God we talked about." Kraft concludes, "The God of power portrayed in the Scriptures seemed to have died."[12]

Kraft's missionary experience was deficient, in part, because of his failure to see God's reign over the demonic spirits which caused so much suffering in Nigeria. This led to a faulty application of Western medicine to a dark spiritual reality. No wonder he records that the natives returned to the medicine man for help as they had formerly done before their conversion. Much later, back in the United States, Kraft began to see people healed not only by medication but by the power of God. This changed his functional worldview and his ministry. Thus, he concludes, "I find myself reading the Bible (especially the Gospels) with new eyes—knowing that miracles and deliverances and revelations from God and angels and demons and all those things I used to read about only as inspired history are for us today! I find a new desire to pray, to talk to God and to listen to him. . . . There is a new power and authority in ministry, as well as a compelling desire to minister to others."[13] Now, for Kraft, the God of power portrayed in the Scriptures no longer seems to have died as he thought in Nigeria, but is alive. With this, Kraft has begun to take on, to use Blamires' phrase, "the Christian mind."

Why is building the Christian mind such a fight? Why are so many people deceived by secular forces? We must now address an essential aspect of revelation: the problem of evil in God's good universe. Our response to God's kingdom has been threatened by a heavenly revolt which has resulted in earthly chaos, and to this we now turn.

FOUR

The Assault of Satan

To grasp the kingdom of God is difficult because our minds are under the attack of an evil force. I am certain that this will surprise many of us because Satan is rarely acknowledged today. The secular world does not believe in a personal evil, such as the one revealed in Scripture. Thus, Christians are often dissuaded from confronting the forces of darkness. Despite two world wars, the holocaust, and antagonistic nuclear arsenals which could turn this planet into a deathstar, we still experience polite disdain when the existence of personal, supernatural evil is proposed as the explanation for our current state of affairs. Along with our intoxication with the myths of human goodness and society's progress, we also suffer from a number of ploys which have given the devil bad press. These include black masses and witchhunts which have now fallen before "the clear light of reason" and modern psychology. So as it turns out, much of our dealing with Satan is a pathological projection of unconscious fears and a surrender of our own moral responsibility as we claim, in the words of Flip Wilson, that "the devil made me do it." We also suffer from our Disney-like fantasies where evil is a literary device for dramatic conflict, easily resolved by a good fairy or a charming prince.

Nevertheless, in this insecure age, we are forced at least to reevaluate whether we have dismissed the devil all too quickly (which may well be his design). Certainly many modern thinkers admit that if there is no personal, supernatural evil, then at least there is a collective evil which is greater than the sum of its parts. This led the German philosopher Paul Tillich to introduce the "category of the demonic" and the French novelist Camus to see Hitler's Germany as that irrational evil which arose from the sewers like rats.

Furthermore, there is a growing body of psychiatric literature which observes evil far beyond its human dimensions. For example, M. Scott Peck, whose *The Road Less Traveled* became a best seller, followed this optimistic guide for spiritual growth with *People of the Lie*. While judging his previous book as "nice," he goes on to say that his new work is not "nice," it is about people who are evil.[1] Moreover, it is also about the devil. As Peck confesses, "While I know Satan to be lustful to penetrate us, I have not in the least experienced this desire as sexual or creative—only hateful and destructive."[2] Along with psychiatric studies, there is also sociological data such as that of Wade Davis of Harvard who discovered in Haiti that spirits are real, that they possess people, and that our scientific tools are useless in evaluating them. After observing a woman holding a live coal in her mouth for three minutes, Davis writes, "The woman had clearly entered some kind of spirit realm. But what impressed me the most was the ease with which she did so. I had no experience or knowledge that would allow me to rationalize or to escape what I had seen."[3]

Perhaps more important than scientific observations are the personal confessions of a man like Malcolm Muggeridge, the former editor of the British humor magazine *Punch*, who ironically admits that he has found it easier to believe in the devil than in God, as he says, "... for one thing, alas, I have had more to do with him." Muggeridge continues:

> It seems to me quite extraordinary that anyone should have failed to notice, especially during the last half century, a

diabolic presence in the world, pulling downwards as gravity does.... A counter-force to creativity; destructive in its nature and purpose, raging far and wide like a forest fire, and burning in the heart's core—pinpointed there, a fiery tongue of fierce desire.... Have we not smelt him rancid sweet? Touched him, slippery soft? Measured with the eye his fearful shape? Heard his fearful rhetoric? Glimpsed him, sometimes in a mirror, with drooling, greedy mouth, misty ravening eyes and flushed flesh? Who can miss him in those blackest of all moments, when God seems to have disappeared, leaving the devil to occupy an empty universe?[4]

The Devil's Masks

As I have already asserted, the biblical worldview is consistently supernatural: nature is controlled by God. At the same time, the biblical worldview is also consistently personal. Evil, therefore, is no abstraction; it is as personal as God himself. For example, when Jesus spoke to demons, they spoke back. However, the Bible shows that while there is a continual supernatural interaction between heaven and earth, the focus is on God's covenant relationship with us rather than on the supernatural as such. For this reason, the Bible never indulges in speculative angelology or demonology. Since biblical history is the history of salvation, angels share this history only as they serve in Yahweh's court or rebel against that court and infect the earth with wickedness. Moreover, since God does not choose to redeem the fallen angels, they merely play a part as instruments of his wrath and are destined to be defeated and judged.

At the same time, despite the absence of a systematic view of evil,[5] the God of the Bible carries on a continual battle with idols and common "folk religion." Thus, Israel is warned not to imitate the "detestable things" of her neighbors when she enters the Promised Land (Dt 18:9). As Moses commands, "There shall not be found among you anyone who makes his son or his daughter pass through the fire [offered as a burnt sacrifice to Molech, see Leviticus 20:2], one who uses divination, one who practices witchcraft, or one who interprets omens, or a sorcerer, or one who casts a spell, or a medium, or a spiritist, or one who calls up the dead" (Dt 18:10-11). Such people are "detestable to the LORD" and are to be driven out (Dt 18:12). Furthermore, no sacrifices are to be made to "goat demons" (Lv 17:7) and mediums or spiritists are to be put to death (Lv 20:27). Moreover, those who turn to them will be cut off by Yahweh (Lv 20:6, see 19:31). For Israel, trafficking in mediums and idols continues to be a real and present danger. David's wife Michal (Saul's daughter) harbors a household idol and uses it to deceive her father (1 Sm 19:13); and in the final crisis of his life King Saul calls upon the witch at Endor who brings Samuel back from the dead (1 Sm 28:7ff). Later, David's son Solomon is turned to idols by his foreign wives (1 Kgs 11:4-8) and, after his death, his kingdom is torn in two as a result of God's judgment (1 Kgs 11:11-13).

The reason for the harsh demands against occult practices and idols is that they are connected to a real evil which will seduce God's people away from him. Their practitioners are agents or channels of spiritual power. For example, I recall having my tea leaves read in a Chinese restaurant in Hawaii some years ago. It was merely entertaining until the hostess who interpreted from my cup began to tell me things out of my past which she had no way of knowing. Suddenly the fun turned to fear as I was touched by dark spirituality. This real power has influenced many toward "New Age" religion, popularized by people such as actress Shirley MacLaine, with their channeled messages from the supernatural realm.[6] Much to the dismay of conservative Christians, this real power also drew Nancy Reagan to a socialite astrologer who ended up advising her on the former President's schedule and travel plans.

Beyond these "harmless" examples stand the communal evil of a Jim Jones, who took hundreds of his followers with him in a death pact, and the active, proselytizing Satanic church with its own priesthood, liturgy, and "Bible." A growing problem for law enforcement in our country also centers in occult practices which include lurid sexual crimes and the mutilation and sacrificing of both animals and children. Here stark violence and evil become overwhelming.

It is no surprise, then, that Israel's continual idolatry provokes prophetic denunciation. For example, God tells the northern kingdom through Hosea:

> My people consult their wooden idol, and their diviner's wand informs them;
> For a spirit of harlotry [a supernatural spirit] has led them astray,
> And they have played the harlot, departing from their God. (Hos 4:12)

Similar words lace Isaiah and Jeremiah. Therefore, when the book of the law is rediscovered, King Josiah (640-609 B.C.) carries out a reform which reaches even to the temple in Jerusalem itself. Cleansing it of vessels made "for Baal, for Asherah, and for all the host of heaven," he removes the Asherah (Caananite mother-goddess) and breaks down the houses of the "male cult prostitutes which were in the house of the LORD" (2 Kgs 23:4-7). All of this evidences the low point to which Israel's faith had sunk. No wonder Isaiah warned that God's people were "filled with influences from the east," including soothsayers and idols (Is 2:6-8), and would now face the "terror of the LORD" (Is 2:10).

This battle against idolatry helps us understand why Israel was in constant conflict with her pagan neighbors. While the idols themselves are nothing since they neither see nor hear nor speak (in contrast to Yahweh), they are something in so far as they mask the demon spirits which lie behind them. As Moses says in Deuteronomy, when God's people succumb to idols, they find themselves bound to supernatural evil: "They sacrificed to demons who were not God, To gods whom they have not known ..." (Dt 32:17). Likewise, in Psalm 106:37 when children are burned before the god Molech, God's people "sacrificed their sons and their daughters to the demons." Israel's wars are theocratic; they are "holy wars," fought against spiritual and political evil. Thus, in making alliances with foreign nations Israel makes alliances with their gods. Since Yahweh demands an exclusive relationship with her, Israel stands under his judgment when she makes pacts with these gods.

One further point is worth noting. Although the Bible engages in a continual polemic against the idols, as revelation progresses, the identity of the spiritual forces behind them becomes clearer. Certainly this is due in part to the influences of apocalyptic literature, but it is also due to the fact that with the Incarnation the devil's hand is forced. Satan's strategy is to disguise himself behind the false fronts of legitimate institutions such as government and religion. Only when God's Son steps into history is Satan then smoked out of hiding. This is his ultimate crisis and he must take the field in his own defense.

Tempter and Deceiver

As we have seen, the Bible views us as locked into a supernatural civil war that determines events on this planet. A revolt before the throne of God, predating Eden, has turned the universe into a battle zone. While Scripture never provides us with a systematic theology of evil, it always presupposes both the original goodness of creation and its primeval disruption. The central figure in this drama is Satan (accuser and slanderer), a magnificent, fallen angel. The few Old Testament references to him become prolific in the New Testament. Starting in Genesis when the serpent tempts Eve, we learn that sin only enters into human history with outside help. Since the heart of temptation is pride, becoming "like God" (Gn 3:5), could this suggestion have come from anyone but God's archenemy who fell from heaven himself because of his presumption? Not according to Revelation where the devil is identified as "the serpent of old who is called the devil and Satan, who deceives the whole world" (Rv 12:9).

This evil, supernatural invasion of our lives becomes even clearer in Genesis 6 when the "sons of God" who quite clearly are fallen angels, marry the daughters of men and have children with them by possessing other humans as their instruments (compare Mark 12:25). This results in a great morass of evil which ends in the virtual destruction of the race by the flood. Such a demonic attack upon the earth rightly presupposes that heaven itself is in discord. This rift now manifests itself here through the vanity of idolatry as the nations worship the works of their hands rather than the Lord God. As we have seen, Israel's battles against her neighbors, then, are wars of religion or theological wars. While Satan may be named only three times in the Old Testament, the effects of his revolt are written boldly across the whole canon through Israel's life and death struggle with the idols, the occult, and their demon powers. But what, we may ask, is his role?

First of all, Satan is the individual tempter. For example, he appears before God and his heavenly court like a prosecuting attorney in order to gain permission to tempt Job (Jb 1:6ff). Second, Satan deceives the whole earth as he commands his fallen angels in the heavenly revolt (Rv 12:7-9). This gives us further evidence that originally he was a highly exalted supernatural being who, according to Job, had access to God's intimate council. Moreover, because of his position of power, he not only rebelled against divine authority, but also took a host of angels with him. They now provide a counter kingdom to God's kingdom, an evil empire hierarchically organized under Satan himself. Thus, Jesus speaks of "the devil and his angels" (Mt 25:41) and is charged by the Pharisees with casting out demons by a pact with the "ruler of the demons" (Mk 3:22).

This evil empire is also described in the Bible as containing principalities and powers. It seems that in creation God gave his angels rule over planets and nations. Thus, in Deuteronomy 32:8, the text reads that God "fixed the borders of the peoples according to the number of the sons of God [the angels]...." Michael Green in his book *I Believe in Satan's Downfall* adds, "The meaning is well brought out elsewhere: Deuteronomy 4:19 speaks of the moon, stars, and hosts of heaven which the Lord has allotted to all the peoples under heaven, with the exception of Israel whom He has appointed for Himself.'" Thus, angelic rulers control the nations, and Yahweh controls them. At the same time, these rulers are now fallen (see Psalm 82). So if earthly kingdoms become corrupt, the angelic rulers could hardly be acquitted of responsibility. This explains why Isaiah can speak an oracle of judgment against the king of Babylon and then shift his address abruptly to "Lucifer," the power behind the king (Is 14:12). Likewise, Ezekiel denounces the prince of Tyre and then makes a lamentation for the king of Tyre, the spiritual ruler over him (Ez 28:12ff). Similarly, in Daniel, aid for God's people is temporarily thwarted by the prince of the kingdom of Persia, an angelic ruler, who is then overcome by the angel Michael. This line of thought, however, is not peculiar to a few Old Testament authors. As we have seen, whenever Israel does battle against pagan nations, she is also locked in combat with their gods and the supernatural powers behind them. War is always theocracy against theocracy. Nothing is "secular"; all is "sacred."

While the details of Satan's fall with his hordes of demon-angels are not specifically given in the Bible, the reality is everywhere assumed. For the New Testament, however, the breaking in of God's kingdom in the ministry of Jesus decisively changes the devil's position in heaven and on earth. Thus, when Jesus' disciples subject demons in his name, he replies, "I was watching Satan fall from heaven like lightning" (Lk 10:18). Furthermore, John reminds us that although "the whole world lies in the power of the evil one" (1 Jn 5:19), yet, the "Son of God appeared ... that He might destroy the works of the devil" (1 Jn 3:8).

We have introduced Satan's assault upon God's reign here in order to complete our picture of Yahweh's heavenly court, accessed by good and evil angels, and in order to understand the presuppositions for the Fall and God's response in redemptive history. As he sits enthroned in glory, surrounded by his cherubim, with his angelic retainers gathered before him, God's reign is now determined by the heavenly/earthly revolt which has decisively changed the destiny of our planet.

As suggested, insight into this history will help us to understand our own culture and its current decay. But the relevance of all of this does not end with mere intellectual comprehension. If this revolt is a part of our reality, it also prepares us for a dramatic change in ministry. For example, Jack Deere, former Associate Professor of Old Testament at Dallas Theological Seminary recounts, "When our church began going through a period of revival, one of the first things that happened was the Holy Spirit revealed the presence of demonic activity within the individuals in our fellowship. I have been involved in eight to ten cases of healing a demonized person."[8]

What this healing means specifically is documented by psychiatrist John White in his recent book, *When the Spirit Comes with Power*. Here he discusses a man named Conrad, a native of Calgary, Alberta, Canada, who was haunted by his seventeen-year addiction to marijuana after becoming a Christian. Although he had repented of his drug use, his sorrow did not deliver him. He admitted, "I simply could not resist temptation." At a healing conference, when encountered by a pastor from Vancouver he blurted out, "Ken, I've been smoking pot for a long time and I want to be free. I want to move on." Ken Blue looked at him and then prayed, "Father, Conrad hasn't really wanted to be free. Take him . . . at his word." Conrad now narrates what happened:

> As he prayed, I felt an absolutely wonderful, powerful stream of what I best envisage as light pouring in through the back of my neck. I began to shake. . . . I felt a tightness in

my chest. It became a convulsion as the power continued to flow in. I began to cough, hack. As this happened the tightness in my chest began to move up through my body and out of my mouth.

This all lasted two to three minutes. As the tightness left and the convulsing ceased, I felt a void within myself. Ken sensed this and prayed that the void would be filled with God, and it was. I had never experienced such energy in my life, and I had experienced many things. I felt almost drunk, and free and powerful. I knew I had been touched by God.... I knew I had been shown another dimension of God's kingdom on earth. I smiled and felt God's glow for hours.

As Conrad was being prayed for, his friend Mark, standing nearby, felt fused with him. He recounts:

I knew, felt, experienced what was going on inside of him. As [Ken's] prayers got more accurate ... closer to what the problem was [a spirit] my body went crazy—very powerful jolts, like electricity—and my whole upper body would nod violently in agreement. My spirit would scream inside me, "Yes! Yes!"

As the prayers got very specific and accurate I no longer "heard" them. I experienced them, and a violent struggle between good and evil rose up inside of me. It was awful, like being torn apart. My friends watching me told me later they saw my face sort of screw up in pain and get red, and they thought I would have a heart attack. The struggle was very real and intense, and then [Ken] commanded the spirit to leave.

Instantly [there came] a flood of peace and I knew it was over. Right when the rip happened [Conrad] fell backward and when I turned and opened my eyes he had the biggest smile I've ever seen. He just grinned and said, "It's gone! It's gone! I feel it, it's gone!" He hasn't done drugs since.[9]

A somewhat similar story comes from my friend, Trey, whose roommate, a professed Christian, was obsessed by chronic suicidal thoughts. He began specifically to plan his own death. Since Trey was a member of a traditional, conservative church he had run through all the standard treatments both spiritual and psychological, but to no avail. Finally, in desperation, he phoned a Pentecostal friend for help as his roommate watched. The friend simply said, "He has a demon of suicide" and asked that Trey put him on the line. He obliged and after thirty seconds his roommate dropped the phone, backed across the room and cried, "It's coming out of me!" "It's coming out of me!" From this point on his obsession with death left.

As these accounts reveal, we are dealing with a real, personal evil which specializes in human bondage and self-destruction. Ministry with such people, which is amply documented in the Gospels, must be understood within the context of the history of Satan's attack upon God and his attack upon God's creation. Let us turn to this history.

FIVE

The Kingdom Revealed, Rejected, and Restored

OUR RECOVERY OF THE CHRISTIAN MIND and a comprehensive view of reality depends on our understanding the biblical worldview. Central to this worldview is that God is the Creator and Sustainer of life—he is King. All the authors of the Bible presuppose this truth. As King, God established a kingdom which appears on our planet in time, space, and history. The primary revelation of this kingdom is in creation. After the Fall disrupted the earth, God reestablished his reign by binding Abraham to himself. That reign is then extended through his heirs as the nations are blessed with the gift of salvation. Let us begin our study of God's kingdom by considering the early chapters of Genesis where the drama of our history unfolds.

In His Image

The Bible opens with the sublime announcement: "In the beginning God created the heavens and the earth" (Gn 1:1). This is the foundation not only of biblical faith but also of Western civilization as we know it. Both the demystification of nature (its forces are not gods, as in paganism) and the biblical sense of God's created order made modern science possible. Since nature was not divine, it could be examined, and because God had made it, it had a structure ("laws of nature") to be unlocked. It is no accident that such science originated in the "Christian" West. Once the biblical worldview was surrendered, however, we were left with the philosophy of meaningless evolution by random chance ("natural selection") rather than a theology of nature under the commanding direction of God's will.

As we have already seen, when God creates from his throne he speaks the heavens and the earth into existence. He commands, " 'Let there be light'; and there was light" (Gn 1:3). Moreover, since God creates out of nothing, matter is temporal rather than eternal. To worship it as modern materialists do (both capitalists and Marxists) is to become an idolater (Rom 1:25). As each day of creation builds upon the next, God's order and purpose drive all things toward their predetermined goal. Indeed, the creation displays his glory (Ps 19:1).

Then God announces, "Let Us make man in Our image, according to Our likeness" (Gn 1:26). The plural, which has confused many, expresses both his formal "throne language," representing his fullness, and his address to the angelic court gathered before him. At the same time, it also reveals the complexity of the one God who lives in eternal fellowship within himself as Father, Son, and Holy Spirit. During the act of creation, God speaks to his Son, his Spirit, and his holy angels. But what does it mean to be made in the "image of God?"

First, since God is a person, he gives us the gift of personality. Second, as persons we also have moral responsibility and eternal value before him. Third, God creates us to live in fellowship with him and reflect his character in this world. Fourth, created in his image as "male and female," we are designed to reflect that image by living together in heterosexual rather than homosexual or unisexual community.

Thus, God gives us both gender identity as either male *or* female and gender roles as male *and* female. He places a special blessing upon our sexuality, commanding us to be fruitful and multiply (Gn 1:28). Thus as God is creative, so we are to be creative. Not only has he given us being and value, he has also given us power.

In the ancient world when a king conquered a territory, he erected a statue of himself within it, showing that the new acquisition now belonged to him. Likewise, God has made us in his image and placed us on this planet to show that it belongs to him. He now delegates his authority and reign to us. As he commands in Genesis 1:26 after our creation, "Let them rule over the fish of the sea and over the birds of the sky and over the cattle and over all the earth." Therefore, our destiny is to exercise divine dominion, to be the agents of his kingdom. We rule because he rules us.

Furthermore, our King provides us with worship, order, prosperity, and security. Our first parents were lovers of God who enjoyed free and open communion with their Creator. God ordered their lives not only by delegating to them his dominion over the creation, but also by demanding that they live under the limits of his law, in this case, represented by the commandment that they not eat of the tree of the knowledge of good and evil. The idyllic setting of the Garden of Eden, surrounded by rushing rivers (Gn 2:10ff) and lavish gems (Gn 2:11-12), suggests that God granted abundant prosperity to his original subjects. Their simple task was to care for his good earth. Eternal security was also theirs since they ruled paradise. Dominion over the animals (who posed no threat) is expressed as Adam names them (Gn 2:19-20). Furthermore, since it was not good for man to be alone, woman was created from him and for him to be his companion and helpmate. Thus, man and woman were to be joined together in a permanent union as "one flesh" (Gn 2:24). The innocence of this time is well represented by the conclusion that they were both naked and unashamed (Gn 2:25). God's kingdom here for one brief shining moment is a happy Camelot. But this soon changes. The dark shadow of Satan reflected through the serpent now appears.

"You Shall Be Like God"

Much theological thought and writing has centered on the Fall in Genesis 3. The crafty serpent, an apt symbol for Satan (compare Revelation 12:9), provides the dynamics of temptation. The sequence of sin's entrance into our world may be summed up by three words: "question," "contradiction," and "deception." To begin with, the serpent questions, "Indeed, has God said, 'You shall not eat from any tree of the garden?'" (Gn 3:1). Eve's mind is now awakened to doubt, to "think for herself." This distancing from innocent faith is then immediately followed by a contradiction. Here, the serpent undermines God's warning that eating from the tree of the knowledge of good and evil will produce death when he says: "You surely shall not die" (Gn 3:4). This denial is now supported by deception, "For God knows that in the day you eat from it your eyes will be opened, and you will be like God, knowing good and evil" (Gn 3:5). It is important for us to understand this sequence because the devil will use the same strategy on us in our war with him. He will get us to question God's Word. He will then deny God's Word, offering us bogus hope.

Eve's invitation to rebellion is now marvelously reinforced by her powers of rationalization: "When the woman saw that the tree was good for food, and that it was a delight to the eyes, and that the tree was desirable to make one wise..." (Gn 3:6). Such justification quickly results in the evil deed: "... she took from its fruit and ate;..." which spreads immediately: "... and she gave also to her husband with her, and he ate" (Gn 3:6). The Fall is complete. Knowing that they are naked, Adam and Eve begin to hide themselves (Gn 3:7). Their hiding among the garden's trees symbolizes their separation from God, and their aprons of fig leaves symbolize their separation from each other. Rather than living in perfect communion with God, each other, and creation, they experience the breakdown of all their relationships. What, then, brought about this disaster?

The Heavenly Fall

As we have seen, rebellion on earth reflects rebellion in heaven. Thus, the devil appeals to our first parents' pride ("You shall be like God"), just as he originally fell by his own pride. This heavenly revolt is suggested in Isaiah's taunt over the king of Babylon and the rebellious angelic ruler who stands behind him:

> How you have fallen from heaven,
> O star of the morning, son of the dawn!
> You have been cut down to the earth,
> You who have weakened the nations!
> But you said in your heart,
> "I will ascend to heaven;
> I will raise my throne above the stars of God,
> And I will sit on the mount of assembly
> In the recesses of the north.
> I will ascend above the heights of the clouds;
> I will make myself like the Most High."
> Nevertheless you will be thrust down to Sheol.
> (Is 14:12-15)

This heavenly fall is even more clearly represented in Ezekiel's lament over the "king" of Tyre, the supernatural ruler over the prince of Tyre (Ez 28:2, 12):

> "You had the seal of perfection,
> Full of wisdom and perfect in beauty.
> You were in Eden, the garden of God . . .
> You were the anointed cherub who covers . . .
> Until unrighteousness was found in you. . . .

> Therefore I have cast you as profane
> From the mountain of God. . . .
> Your heart was lifted up because of your beauty;
> You corrupted your wisdom by reason of your splendor."
> (Ez 28:12-17)

In both of these texts pride is asserted as the cause of this heavenly fall. As the "star [angel] of the morning" says, "I will make myself like the Most High" and as Ezekiel accuses the "king" of Tyre ("the anointed cherub"), "Your heart was lifted up because of your beauty." Satanic and human pride ("You shall be like God") usurp God's kingdom and lead to his judgment. As Isaiah warns, "For the LORD of hosts will have a day of reckoning Against everyone who is proud and lofty, And against everyone who is lifted up, That he may be abased" (Is 2:12). On this day the ultimate egotist, the devil himself, will also be cast into the lake of fire forever (Rv 20:10).

If pride is the reason for Satan's fall, how does pride motivate Satan to attack us? Why does he seduce us away from God's kingdom? Because God has created us in his image and given us dominion over this planet, it is the devil's purpose to usurp our dominion and expand his evil empire by gaining us. As Adam and Eve yielded to the serpent's temptation, they rejected God's kingdom for the illusion of having their own. Then they lost everything. The world, designed to be ruled by them, was stolen by the devil. That he has been successful is seen not only in the Old Testament by the bitter battles which Israel fought with her demon-dominated neighbors, but also in the New Testament when Satan offered Jesus the kingdoms of this world (Mt 4:8-9). Here again the devil's ploy is clear. For the price of a simple act of worship, Jesus may get earthly kingdoms, but the devil will get Jesus, and in getting him he will get everything.

God now comes walking in his garden in the cool of the day, looking for those entrusted with its care (Gn 3:8). After discovering Adam and Eve in hiding, he interrogates them as the just Judge and then pronounces his sentence upon them (Gn 3:11-19). By his decree, the serpent must crawl on his belly as a sign of Satan's humiliation. Moreover, his final doom is assured when God pronounces that the woman's seed or heir (which is ultimately Jesus) will crush his head (Gn 3:15, compare Romans 16:20). The woman will also have pain in childbirth (new life is now a mixed blessing), and be dominated by her husband (male domination is a part of the curse). In turn, the man will sweat out his living from the devastated earth until he returns to its dust.

Expelled from the garden by Yahweh's just judgments, man and woman now live "east of Eden." The gates are closed and access is guarded by a flaming sword and angels sent from God's heavenly court (Gn 3:24). From this point the sorry human history of murder, demonic possession, and resulting violence unfolds. Genesis 6:5 concludes that "the wickedness of man was great on the earth, and . . . every intent of the thoughts of his heart was only evil continually." But God is not passive before all this. He is no divine clockmaker who winds up everything and lets it run. Neither is he a mystical "high" into which we may escape. He continues to reign over the earth as the just Judge. Thus, as he interrogated Adam and Eve after the Fall, he now interrogates Cain over the death of his brother and then judges him (Gn 4:9-12). Moreover, through his Spirit he strives with mankind (Gn 6:3) and exercises his reign in signs and wonders by flooding the earth because of its corruption (Gn 6-9). Here we see that the planet is accountable to him and that nature is at his command (Gn 7:11-12; 8:1-2). Later, when mankind attempts to reach heaven by constructing the tower of Babel, God breaks the assault by confusing the common language of the workers (Gn 11:1-9).

While the major themes of our early history in Genesis 1-11 are sin and judgment, the minor themes of God's providence and protection also appear. For example, God provides animal skins as a covering for Adam and Eve when they are expelled from Eden (Gn 3:21). Moreover, after killing his brother, Cain also receives divine protection while he wanders alone (Gn 4:15). Then, God saves a remnant in righteous Noah and his family, giving them specific directions for preparing and filling the ark with representative animals as they ride out the deluge (Gn 6:18ff). Later, the rainbow is given as the sign of God's covenant promise never again to turn the earth into a watery grave (Gn 9:1ff). His reign is not one of "passive paternalism." God is the active, sovereign King. While we can certainly understand why he judges the earth, the real question is: "Why does he preserve the earth?" The answer lies in his purpose to restore his kingdom despite Satan's usurpation and our sin. This restoration begins with Abraham and the unfolding of redemptive history.

The Kingdom Restored

God's kingdom now breaks in upon Abram, a Mesopotamian whose roots lie in the Sumerian city of Ur (Gn 11:27-32). God calls Abram to abandon his past, his country, his relatives, and his father's house (Gn 12:1). By implication, this radical break also includes abandoning the old polytheistic theocracy which, as we have seen, was the context within which he worshiped and lived. From now on Yahweh will reign over Abram as his King rather than the gods of Ur and extend the kingdom of God through his line as he is given a new land and becomes a great nation (Gn 12:1-2). Moreover, Abram will become a blessing to those who bless him. At the same time, those who curse him will be cursed (Gn 12:3). He is not called to a narrow nationalism, but to the world as the agent of God's reign: "And in you all the families of the earth shall be blessed" (Gn 12:3).

God summons a single man into history, giving him a destiny far greater than Abram could imagine. With this call before Abram, much to our amazement, he abandons his old life and his old identity and begins the long migration west toward Canaan, following the trade routes still traversed by camels today. It is impossible to overstate the importance of this event for the destiny of the race. As a result of Abram's sheer faith (see Genesis 15:6) and the obedience which demonstrates it, God now makes a covenant with him. His relationship with Abram can only be understood in light of that covenant, which, in turn, can only be understood in light of God as King.

The Abrahamic covenant reflects the treaties which Hittite kings made with their favored retainers. These treaties were called "royal grants" and were given to special counselors or military leaders who had served them well. They were always imposed upon an inferior by a superior and came with rights and privileges for the recipient. Moreover, the royal grant was unconditional, perpetual, and usually included the gift of a city or a large estate. The king himself guaranteed that the grant would be honored. Thus, a Hittite king says to his vassal, "After you, your son and grandson will possess it [a gift of land]; nobody will take it away from them. If one of your descendants sins, the king will prosecute him . . . but nobody will take away either his house or his land in order to give it to a descendant of somebody else."[1]

The enactment of the covenant comes in two parts. The first part centers in the promise of a land which will become God's special realm. Thus, in Genesis 15:7 after pledging Abram an heir from his own loins, God assures him, "I am the LORD who brought you out of Ur of the Chaldeans, to give you this land to possess it." The second part of the covenant centers in the gift of a dynasty. Here Abram, who in his old age has no heir, is assured that he will become a great nation. In granting this Yahweh appears again to him announcing: "I am God Almighty," commanding him, "Walk before Me, and be blameless." This is followed by the promise, "And I will establish My covenant [treaty] between Me and you, And I will multiply you exceedingly." In response, Abram assumes the proper posture before a great King by falling on his face (Gn 17:1-3).

God now promises that Abram will produce "a multitude of nations," changing his name to "Abraham" (father of a multitude), and reaffirming the land grant given in Genesis 15, "I will give to you and to your descendants ... all the land of Canaan, for an everlasting possession" (Gn 17:5-8). The covenant is then sealed by circumcision, which should probably be understood in the context of those Near Eastern kings who branded their slaves with a physical mark of ownership. Circumcision would then signify that Abraham and his seed belong to Yahweh as the subjects of his kingdom.

God establishes his gracious rule over Abraham. The use of the covenant as the means for this is unique to Israel's faith and is the appropriate symbol for her exclusive loyalty to Yahweh. In this covenant God proves beyond a doubt that he is King and that his kingdom has come into this fallen world. But what is the content of that kingdom?

Since Yahweh is King, we can expect him to provide worship, order, prosperity, and security for Abraham. Thus, Abraham worships God throughout his lifetime, leaving Canaan dotted with altars (Gn 12:7-8; 13:18). In this he responds to the direct appearance of Yahweh (Gn 12:7), calling upon "the name of the LORD," as the expression of his relationship with his God and his subjection to him (Gn 12:8). Moreover, there are also those moments when Abraham responds spontaneously to God's intervention in his life. For example, he provides hospitality for Yahweh and his angels, offering food and drink (Gn 18:1ff). In return, because of their mutual relationship, God refuses to withhold from Abraham what he is about to do in judging Sodom and Gomorrah. Like a rug merchant in the Cairo bazaar, Abraham then barters with him to spare the cities for the sake of his nephew Lot and his family who live there (Gn 18:17ff).

The summit of Abraham's personal relationship with God comes when God commands him to take his only son and sacrifice him on Mount Moriah as a burnt offering (Gn 22:1ff). Here Abraham's faith and obedience are supremely tested, since all of his hopes for the future are centered in this young boy who is his only heir. As he lifts the knife to kill Isaac, however, God sends an angel to interrupt him. He has passed the test; all that he has, including his only son, belongs to Yahweh. Now a substitute sacrifice is provided, a ram caught in the thicket. After the animal is slaughtered, God then sends his angel a second time to bless Abraham and reconfirm the covenant: "'By Myself I have sworn,'[2] declares the LORD, 'because you have done this thing, and have not withheld your son, your only son, indeed I will greatly bless you, and I will greatly multiply your seed.... And in your seed all the nations of the earth shall be blessed...'" (Gn 22:16-18). In this ultimate act of worship, everything is taken from Abraham and then everything is given back.

Furthermore, since God is King, he is also responsible to provide Abraham with *justice*. Abraham knows him as the "Judge of all the earth" because of his moral character (Gn 18:25). In turn, God expects Abraham to display that character to the world. Thus, he says, "I have chosen [Abraham], in order that he may command his children and his household after him to keep the way of the LORD by doing righteousness and justice." (Gn 18:19). Here the kingdom of God becomes practical as Abraham obeys God. Rather than teaching righteousness by codified law or biblical principles, God teaches (much as we do our children) through the things that happen in Abraham's life. For example, God reveals the importance of marital faithfulness by judging Pharaoh for taking Abraham's wife into his harem (Gn 12:10-20).

God also reveals his character through his dealings with Sodom and Gomorrah. Since he is the just Judge, he agrees with Abraham to save these notorious cities from destruction if a righteous remnant can be found within them. He sends a team of angels to investigate Sodom (Gn 19:1ff). There they are threatened with homosexual rape, violating the law of hospitality and God's order for the sexes given in Genesis 1. After this outrage, the doom of Sodom and Gomorrah is sealed. Yahweh, who commands nature, now pours fire and brimstone, his signs and wonders, down upon the cities from heaven (Gn 19:24). In these judgments God reveals that he is the Judge to whom all people are accountable. Moreover, he molds Abraham's character as he executes his wrath, teaching him to live under the authority of his kingdom.

Furthermore, God brings *blessing* and *bounty* to Abraham. He becomes a man of great possessions (Gn 12:5): "Now Abram was very rich in livestock, in silver and in gold" (Gn 13:2). This only increases throughout his lifetime (see Genesis 12:16; 20:14). In fact, he is so rich that he is forced to separate from his nephew Lot in order to pasture and water his herds (Gn 13:6). Further signs of God's royal blessings are seen in his covenant promise of the gift of the land and the gift of an heir when he makes aged Sarah's womb fruitful (Gn 21:2). These blessings climax in Abraham's living out his years to old age. As Genesis reports, "the LORD had blessed Abraham in every way" (Gn 24:1) and concludes, "And these are all the years of Abraham's life that he lived, one hundred and seventy-five years. And Abraham breathed his last and died in a ripe old age, an old man and satisfied with life; and he was gathered to his people" (Gn 25:7-8). Indeed, in the midst of many battles and a lonely sojourn, the bounty of God's kingdom has been Abraham's.

Along with justice and material prosperity, Yahweh also provides Abraham with *security* by intervening on his behalf. Thus, as we have seen, he delivers his wife Sarah from Pharaoh and later from King Abimelech. Through Abraham God rescues Lot from captivity. Upon Abraham's return from the ensuing military campaign, Melchizedek, the king of Salem, says to him, "... blessed be God Most High, Who has delivered your enemies into your hand" (Gn 14:20). Here God is the Warrior-King who saves his servant from enemies, securing him in his kingdom.

When God calls Abraham and establishes his covenant with him, God manifests his reign to him and through him. Starting with his call, Abraham experiences the divine King's supernatural interventions in his life. God not only speaks his word, he also comes in person to Abraham, sending his angels, pouring out his judgments, granting his bounty, providing his protection, and performing his miracles, such as the birth of Isaac. In return, Abraham submits to God as a subject and slave. Moreover, through all of this Abraham becomes intimate with God. He not only worships him as his King, but also argues with him as his friend. It is no wonder that the promises of God are met with both faith and laughter when he is assured of a son in old age. Thus, it is not Abraham who is glorified here but the God who works through him, molding his life and directing his circumstances in the inauguration of redemptive history.

Throughout the rest of Genesis, God's unconditional covenant with Abraham is reconfirmed to his heirs (compare Genesis 26:2-5, 24; 28:13-15). Moreover, God's supernatural visitations continue as he speaks his living word and sends divine dreams and angelic messengers in order to direct the destiny of the patriarchs. Genesis concludes, then, with Abraham's grandson Jacob and his family sojourning in Egypt. This sets the stage for the signs and wonders of the Exodus, the great Old Testament event of redemptive history.

"Leave All and Follow Me"

The thesis that God is King holds the early traditions of Israel together. From creation to covenant, her history now makes sense in the light of God's reign. Moreover, God's larger purpose in calling Abraham and reversing the effects of the Fall is now revealed. The Creator-King will establish his reign throughout this whole rebellious planet. At the same time, in God's special relationship with Abraham, we see the radical nature of this reign: It is all or nothing. Abraham, therefore, is called to abandon his past, to be bound to an exclusive covenant, a "royal grant" with the living God. Moreover, this covenant also represents true monotheism. Stripped of everything, Abraham now lives solely by faith in the one God.

Accordingly, his hope for an heir is tested. When his and his wife's body are as good as dead, he is finally given the desire of his heart—Isaac is born. Later, as we have seen, God demands Isaac back as a sacrifice on the altar. Such is God's kingdom. He will rule everything or else! This, of course, foreshadows the consummation of his kingdom when He will be "all in all" (1 Cor 15:28).

In Abraham, then, God manifests his reign. Through him the kingdom revealed in creation and rejected by Adam and Eve is restored and begins its advance. Thus, Abraham is blessed not only for his sake but also for our sake as well. We see God's missionary heart as he rolls back the kingdom of darkness and seeks his lost creation. No wonder Paul asserts that the Abrahamic covenant stands throughout all the vicissitudes of Israel's history as the proper foundation for God's ultimate salvation blessing in his Son (Gal 3:14). Furthermore, Abraham's radical trust in God makes him our example as a man of faith. Like those who believe in Christ today, he is counted as righteous not because of his works or the sign of circumcision, but because he takes God at his word and believes him without reservation (see Romans 4). For this reason, we have no less a calling than to be like father Abraham.

God still works with us today as he did with Abraham. He is still the sovereign Lord. His demands are still radical and his tests severe. Jesus confirms this when he calls us to deny ourselves, take up our cross and follow him (Mk 8:34). As Dietrich Bonhoeffer aptly comments, "When Jesus calls a man He bids him come and die."[3]

Carol Wimber recounts such a "death" experience when, after being an elder and a teacher in a church which denied that the gifts of the Holy Spirit are for today, she awakened one night speaking in tongues. In shock, Carol entered a period of intense self-evaluation. She writes,

> I had gone to God asking Him what was wrong with the church, and He was showing me what was wrong with me.

... I was so devastated that I stopped teaching, resigned from the church board, and stopped giving my opinion about anything spiritual. I abandoned all that I had been devoted to for so long and hid out at home for three weeks, weeping and repenting of my attitude toward God and His Spirit. Today I look back on that experience as a "personality meltdown," a breaking of my self-will that was so profound I have never been the same since.[4]

Likewise, Tom Stipe, a pastor in Denver, Colorado, tells of his early Christian life in the "Jesus Movement" where he experienced the power of God. Nevertheless, as time passed, this became distant to him. On a hunting trip in the Rockies, however, he had what he describes as a "visitation." Stipe writes,

The Spirit of the Lord came upon me in the most fearsome way that I could ever describe. Once I was alone, the Spirit began to bring up some of the areas of conviction that He had been speaking to me about. He was stern! . . . I felt as though the Lord was saying, "Are you going to serve Me? I saved your life. If you are not going to serve Me, I may as well take you home." I was convinced at that moment that if I had not recommitted my ministry to the Lord, that I would not have come down that mountain.[5]

God has dealt with me through "death experiences" more than once. The most recent one was when the church which I served as pastor was ripped from me. As we entered a period of renewal, I had assumed that God would use my ministry and that of our church to touch the larger Presbyterian denomination and be a model of a congregation which had come alive in the Holy Spirit. But, as Jesus says, a house divided against itself cannot stand, and the time came when, much to my dismay and to the surprise of the congregation, the elders asked me to resign. As I went home in shock, the Lord said,

"It's off the wall, don't fight it; its me." Like Abraham I was called to raise the knife over my Isaac and trust the provision of God.

Indeed, God's reign is still all or nothing, and it is exactly for that reason that he demanded Israel back from Pharaoh in the Exodus.

SIX

Kingdom Power

AS THE HOLY MOUNTAIN BELCHES FIRE AND SMOKE, Yahweh descends and holds court with Israel gathered below. The account of how God's people came to Sinai, what they did there, and their journey onward stands at the heart of the Old Testament. The irrevocable decisions made at Sinai determine Israel's future and our future as well. Here the sovereign King enacts a new covenant with his people, establishing the law, the priesthood, the tabernacle, and the sacrificial system. He gives them a new identity, molding a people after his own character, incorporating them into his kingdom, giving them the very law which continues to form our basic moral sense some 3400 years later.

Yahweh Goes to War

The Book of Genesis ends with God's people far from the Promised Land. Joseph, Abraham's great-grandson, is sold by his brothers into slavery in Egypt. There he achieves the position of second-in-command under Pharaoh and later saves his family from a famine which forces their migration (Gn 37-50). Israel's favored position, her legacy from Joseph, is then revoked by a dynastic change (Ex 1:8). Reduced to slavery, Israel provides forced labor for Pharaoh's vast building program (Ex 1:11). Moreover, her spiraling population growth threatens Egypt much as the growth of the native Palestinian population threatens Israel today. As a result, she suffers under an edict requiring the death of newborn male children (Ex 1:16).

We must understand that Israel's enslavement was as much religious as it was economic and political. Egypt was a theocracy with Pharaoh as its god-king. Submission to him meant submission to his divine authority. Behind the pagan gods of Egypt, as we have seen, were real spiritual powers (compare Deuteronomy 32:16-17). Where was Yahweh in the midst of this oppression? His rule seemed overturned by the Egyptian crown, his honor violated. However, he hears the cries of his people, remembers his "royal grant" to Abraham (which promised him a land and a dynasty), and takes action (Ex 2:23-25).

One of the most important responsibilities of a king is to go to war on behalf of his subjects. When they are taken captive, he must retrieve them. Otherwise, his treaty is void and he will be mocked. Since God's covenant with Abraham is unconditional, he is honor bound to come to Israel's rescue. In doing this he also vindicates his name. Thus, we are not to be surprised that Yahweh battles against Egypt with his signs and wonders. As King he redeems his people from their slavery to the Egyptian gods (human and divine) and restores his rightful rule over them.

To accomplish this, God called Moses to serve him. Raised by Pharaoh's daughter, he is the perfect choice, knowing the language, the culture, and the court. In the providence of God as a small child, his Israelite mother nursed him, and through her he undoubtedly received his Hebrew identity and his knowledge of the one, true, living God (see Exodus 2:1-10).

In exile, after murdering an Egyptian (Ex 2:11-15), Moses is confronted by God through "the angel of the LORD" whose fiery appearance takes form in a bush at Horeb (Sinai), "the mountain of God" (Ex 3:1). God's call is personal, "Moses,

Moses" (Ex 3:4), and awesome, "...remove your sandals...for the place on which you are standing is holy ground" (Ex 3:5). God announces that he has come to deliver his people from the "power" (literally, the "hand") of the Egyptians and give them the Promised Land (Ex 3:8). Next, he reveals his divine name, "I AM WHO I AM." He is the God who is personal ("I") and eternally present ("AM"). He vows to bring Israel back to this holy mountain where she will worship him as proof that he is the one who has set her free (Ex 3:12).

Since God knows that Pharaoh will not release the Hebrews easily, in violation of our "liberal" sensitivities, he declares war: "So I will stretch out My hand, and strike Egypt with all my miracles which I shall do in the midst of it; and after that he will let you go" (Ex 3:20). The land, then, will literally be sieged by God. Moreover, to prove to Israel that he has called Moses, God gives him authenticating signs: his staff thrown on the ground becomes a serpent, his hand placed in his bosom becomes leprous, and water drawn from the Nile becomes blood on dry ground (Ex 4:3-9). Supported by Aaron his brother, who will compensate for a speech impediment, Moses is now sent to confront the god-king Pharaoh on Yahweh's behalf.

In this call, Moses becomes the archetypal "charismatic leader." Without genealogy or office, he is summoned by the sovereign King into service and given one supreme promise: "I will be with you" (Ex 3:12). No wonder the Book of Numbers asserts that it is the Holy Spirit resting upon Moses who fills his mouth with God's word (Num 11:25). That word for Pharaoh will be clear and concise: "Let My people go, that they may serve Me" (Ex 7:16).

God Backs Up His Act

As the living God assaults Egypt with the plagues, he proves that he is both the Warrior-King who saves his people and the just Judge who comes against the oppressor. Yahweh's goal is not merely to gain political freedom for Israel (as some liberationist theologians believe). He acts in order to bring her under his sovereignty and to destroy the idolatrous system of Egypt (which masks the evil one). For this cause he goes into battle.

Exodus 5-12 recount the mighty acts of God, his signs and wonders which fall like the London Blitz. Here is an authentic "power encounter," which is a visible, practical demonstration that God is more powerful than the gods of Egypt. He promises to strike Egypt with his miracles. The word "miracle" identifies an extraordinary, marvelous deed. Its synonym, "wonder," denotes a direct act of God which provokes awe. By hardening Pharaoh's heart, God creates the context within which he can, as he says, "multiply My signs and My wonders in the land of Egypt" (Ex 7:3). Let us see now how his divine strategy unfolds.

Returning from exile, Moses first secures his base of operations, like a modern insurgent, by gathering the elders of Israel and performing "the signs in the sight of the people." In response they "believed . . . bowed low and worshiped" (Ex 4:30-31). With this support, Moses turns to Pharaoh and presents God's ultimatums in a series of dramatic encounters. His words are verified by his works; the plagues fall with increasing intensity.

The first plague, a kind of chemical warfare, turns the Nile into blood (Ex 7:14-25). Next, a swarm of frogs litter the land (Ex 8:1-15). These miracles, however, are duplicated by Pharaoh's magicians "with their secret arts" (Ex 8:7), showing that this "power encounter" against the dominion of Satan is real.[1] Next, God sends a swarm of gnats which overwhelms the magicians, forcing them to leave the field (Ex 8:16-19). A plague of insects follows (Ex 8:20-32). Next, a kind of germ warfare, a "very severe pestilence," destroys the livestock (Ex 9:1-7) and, then, boils cover man and beast (Ex 9:8-12). This is followed by a violent storm with "hail and fire [lightening]" (Ex 9:24). A horde of locusts now devours whatever is left (Ex

10:1-20). Through all of this, much to our surprise, Pharaoh refuses to capitulate. God, however, uses his hard heart to display his "signs" (Ex 10:1) for the sake of generations to come. As he says, "... that you may tell in the hearing of your son, and of your grandson, how I made a mockery of the Egyptians, and how I performed My signs among them; that you may know that I am the LORD" (Ex 10:2). After this, the sun, held to be a god by the Egyptians, is blotted out and darkness covers the land for three days (Ex 10:21-29).

The plagues now climax in the death of the firstborn. As God says to Moses, "For I will go through the land of Egypt on that night, and will strike down all the first-born in the land of Egypt, both man and beast; and against all the gods of Egypt I will execute judgments—I am the LORD" (Ex 12:12). In what looks like a mistake in the text, Israel herself is also threatened by this plague. Nevertheless, we learn here that even God's chosen people stand under this judgment (all sinners deserve to die). At the same time, God makes a special provision for them by providing a substitute in the passover lambs (Ex 12). After the lambs are sacrificed, Israel is to mark her doorposts with their blood and divine judgment will pass her by. God, however, kills the firstborn of Egypt that night. Finding his land in shambles and the heir to his throne dead, Pharaoh has enough and sends God's people on their way.

Israel is now free from the spiritual and political oppression of Egypt. Loaded with plunder, God leads her to Sinai with a pillar of cloud by day and a pillar of fire by night. The "angel of God," sent from his heavenly court, is also with her (Ex 13:21; 14:19). But once Israel has departed, again God hardens Pharaoh's heart, and prepares to land the crowning blow (Ex 14:4). Gathering his elite chariots, Pharaoh begins a hot pursuit. With this land armada behind them and the sea before them, God's people cry out bitterly to Yahweh. But Moses promises, "The LORD will fight for you while you keep silent" (Ex 14:14). And God splits the waters in front of Israel and brings his people through on dry land. Pharaoh follows, only to see the wall of water collapse upon him, drowning his best troops (Ex 14:28).

Safely on the far shore, Moses and the people sing of Yahweh's mighty conquest. Their theme rings: God is King; he is salvation (Ex 15:2). Moreover, because he is King, "The LORD is a warrior" (Ex 15:3) who has won the battle: "Thy right hand, O LORD, is majestic in power, Thy right hand, O LORD, shatters the enemy" (Ex 15:6). Since nature is also at his command, the wind that piled up the waters is described as the blast of his nostrils (Ex 15:8). Therefore, Israel asks,

> Who is like Thee among the gods, O LORD?
> Who is like Thee, majestic in holiness,
> Awesome in praises, working wonders?
> Thou didst stretch out Thy right hand,
> The earth swallowed them. (Ex 15:11-12)

The song now concludes with this basic confession: "The LORD shall reign forever and ever" (Ex 15:18).

Is this God, the Warrior-King, consistent with the God you worship? Can he unleash his power and decimate the rebellious earth? Will he come with his arm bared to dethrone human pride and set the captives free? Is he in a continuing battle with the forces of darkness, even when they are masked behind religious ideologies and political empires? Does he still command history? Or have you embraced a "lesser god," benevolent, perhaps, but unarmed and defenseless against supernatural evil and its historical incarnations? The account of the Exodus should jolt us. It should leave us breathless before God's holy wrath. But it should allure us as well. This is a God worthy of our worship. This is a God who comes in power because he is faithful to his covenant, and his relentless love for his people will not be denied.

The sovereign King honors his royal treaty with Abraham by going to war with Pharaoh. In so doing, he proves himself faithful to his word given to Abraham to deliver his people (see

Genesis 15:16). As he promised Moses, Israel is now led to Sinai (Horeb) as the sign of her deliverance. Here God comes down from heaven to make a new covenant with his people.

The Making of a People

Enveloped in darkness, with thunder, lightening, and the sound of the trumpet, Yahweh sets up his court before the ragtag multitude of Israel (Ex 19:18). He establishes through this display his supreme "otherness," his separation from all that is unclean or profane. The holy God, hidden in glory, is ready to strike anyone dead who affronts his presence (Ex 19:21-24). His holiness, however, is not just primitive power; it is determined by his moral character and his covenant mercy. Thus, God has proven himself gracious and faithful to his promise by redeeming Israel through his signs and wonders. Now the Warrior-King becomes the lawgiver, the just Judge over his vassal people. What Israel needs is internal order and a national identity. The law gives moral structure while the priesthood, the sacrificial system, and the tabernacle give her identity. Here Israel receives her culture, the rich social life that constitutes a people, her customs, styles, tastes, festivals, rituals—all that unifies individuals socially, morally, and spiritually. For God's people, this happened at Sinai.

God makes a covenant with Israel modeled upon similar Hittite treaties in the Ancient Near East. The Mosaic covenant, however, is unlike the Abrahamic covenant in at least two respects. It is made between God and the nation rather than between God and an individual, and it is conditional rather than unconditional. Thus, while the covenant with Abraham is modeled on the "royal grant," the covenant with Israel is modeled on the "vassal treaty," which is imposed by a king or suzerain upon a conquered people. In it he promises to take his vassal under his protection and, in return, grants certain rights and privileges. At the same time, the covenant has to be observed faithfully.[2]

The giving of the law is central to the covenant. As Judge, God establishes his treaty stipulations and legislates Israel's moral order. This is first given in the Decalogue (Ex 20:1-17), which is followed by a series of case laws revealing that Yahweh is to be the sovereign Lord over all of Israel's life. The supreme expression of his absolute claims, however, stands in the timeless Ten Commandments.

The first commandment addresses the exclusive relationship God has with his people: "You shall have no other gods before Me" (Ex 20:3). The second commandment prohibits idols. They are not to be manufactured, worshiped, or served (Ex 20:4-5). Thus, the people are to submit to God alone in a pure theocracy. In the third commandment, they are not to invoke God's name "in vain," (Ex 3:7) and in the fourth commandment they are to honor him by keeping a Sabbath rest, one day in seven, reflecting his rest on the seventh day of creation (see Genesis 2:2; Exodus 20:8-11). God's people are to mirror his activity in this world. They are to work as he worked and rest as he rested. Imitating him is the rhythm for life.

While the first four commandments deal with Israel's relationship with God, the next six deal with the people's relationships with each other (Ex 20:12-17). The fifth commandment calls them to honor their parents, upholding the family structure. The sixth, calls the people to guard human life as sacred and not take it illegally. The seventh prohibits adultery, upholding the marriage bond. Property rights are secured by the eighth commandment. Truth (especially in a legal context) is to be upheld according to the ninth commandment, and coveteousness (greed) rejected according to the tenth.

Were these absolute demands to stand alone, God's people would grovel under condemnation, impotent and immobilized in their sins before the thundering from the mountain. So, God provides mediated access into his presence through leaders such as Moses, Aaron, and the priesthood, and he establishes the tabernacle and the sacrificial system in order to deal with the results of disobedience (see Exodus 25-31). While Israel is called primarily to worship God by bowing before him in submission, she is also called to bring him offerings and sacrifices. These include burnt offerings which, like tribute paid to a king, are wholly his and, therefore, put to the torch. Moreover, since God's people are sinners, provision is made for the sacrificial (substitutionary) removal of their sins in the Levitical laws. This includes not only regular bloody offerings but also special offerings made once a year by the high priest on the Day of Atonement (Lv 16). Clearly the sacrificial system prepares Israel for the coming of the Messiah, who, in John the Baptist's words, is the "Lamb of God who takes away the sin of the world" (Jn 1:29). Worship, then, is structured with weekly Sabbath observances and a series of annual festivals which recall God's mighty acts and celebrate his material blessings. From Sinai Israel's long education in the ways of God now begins. The law creates moral sensibility and sacrifices remove its consequences by covering and cleansing sin. All of this ultimately ends at the cross, where, as Luther says, God's holiness and love "kiss."

A Stiff-Necked People

Israel's dark, rebellious heart is revealed every step of the way in the Exodus. As Moses laments, he leads a "stiffnecked" people. No wonder that in his absence Aaron is pressured to make a golden calf for an orgy (Ex 32:1). That Israel later refuses to enter the Promised Land after a reconnaissance team reports giants is also no surprise (Nm 14:1ff). When God responds in anger at such unbelief with fire and plague, Moses finds himself interceding again and again for the people. At the same time, God continues to grant Israel his presence, signified by his angel (Ex 32:34), the pillar of cloud (Ex 33:9), and the descending "glory of the LORD" (Ex 40:34). This manifest presence makes Israel unique. No wonder Moses (unlike much of our modern church) refuses to move without it:

> For how then can it be known that I have found favor in Thy sight, I and Thy people? Is it not by Thy going with us, so that we, I and Thy people, may be distinguished from all the other people who are upon the face of the earth? (Ex 33:16)

Throughout the Exodus, God continues to reveal himself directly and supernaturally as Israel's worldview is shaped by her experience of God as King. He comes not only in stern judgments but also in caring provision as he sends manna and quail from heaven and water from the rock (Ex 16-17). Thus, it is Israel who has seen "My glory and My signs, which I performed in Egypt and the wilderness" (Num 14:22). It is also Israel who will experience greater wonders than these when she enters the Promised Land. As God tells Moses,

> Before all your people I will perform miracles which have not been produced in all the earth, nor among any of the nations; and all the people among whom you live will see the working of the LORD, for it is a fearful thing that I am going to perform with you.... I am going to drive out the Amorite before you, and the Canaanite, the Hittite, the Perizzite, the Hivite and the Jebusite. (Ex 34:10-11)

These miracles now are God's instruments of war, bringing his judgment upon the idolatrous nations and extending his reign, his kingdom, through his people as he secures his realm for them.

What are we to make of the signs and wonders in the Exodus? As we have seen, God strikes Egypt in response to the cries of his people (Ex 2:24-25). Since his motive here is not revelation alone but redemption, his power is employed for the sake of his covenant love (Ex 3:7-8, 16; 15:13). Moreover, in the assault, God breaks Pharaoh and the demonic idolatry masked by him, proving that he alone is God. Thus, he says, "The Egyptians shall know that I am the LORD, when I stretch out My hand ... and bring out the sons of Israel from their midst" (Ex 7:5). Again, his motive is not simply revelation alone but judgment. In showing Egypt that Yahweh is King, God also shows that Pharaoh is not. These signs and wonders do not merely prove revelation or accompany revelation as many theologians believe, they *are* revelation. God shows himself to be King by a real victory *over* Egypt. Furthermore, he shows himself to be King by a real victory *for* Israel. His work is to be interpreted by his Word. The two are inseparable.

When God speaks, things happen! Signs and wonders are part of the very nature of God as King. They prevent his reign from being kicked into the "upper storey" of modern theology, like some mental exercise without practical value. Judgment and redemption are events, and they will be felt on earth as God's kingdom breaks in on us. In light of this, we can see why miracles are essential to Jesus' announcement that the kingdom of God is at hand, and why we can expect miracles to verify our announcement of this kingdom as well.

"It's Me"

Does God still manifest his power, holiness, and love in signs and wonders today? Of course, he does. Here is the witness of Carol Wimber:

> On Mother's Day of 1981 we had a watershed experience that launched us into what today is called power evangelism. At this time John [Wimber] invited a young man who had been attending our church to preach on a Sunday evening. By now we had grown to over 700 participants. The young man shared his testimony, which was beautiful and stirring, then asked for all the people under the age of twenty-five to come forward. None of us had a clue as to what was going to

happen. When they got to the front the speaker said, "For years now the Holy Spirit has been grieved by the Church, but he's getting over it. Come Holy Spirit."

And He came.

Most of these young people had grown up around our home—we had four children between the ages of fifteen and twenty-one. We knew the young people well. One fellow, Tim, started bouncing. His arms flung out and he fell over, but one of his hands accidentally hit a mike stand and he took it down with him. He was tangled up in the cord, with the mike next to his mouth. Then he began speaking in tongues, so the sound went throughout the gymnasium [where they were meeting]. We had never considered ourselves charismatics, and certainly had never placed emphasis on the gift of tongues. We had seen a few people tremble and fall over before, and we had seen many healings. But this was different. The majority of the young people [over 400] were shaking and falling over. At one point it looked like a battlefield scene, bodies everywhere, people weeping, wailing, speaking in tongues. And Tim in the middle of it all babbling into the microphone. There was much shouting and loud behavior!

John sat by quietly, playing the piano and wide-eyed. Members of our staff were fearful and angry. Several people got up and walked out, never to be seen again—at least they were not seen by us.

But I knew that God was visiting us. I was so thrilled, because I had been praying for power for so long. This might not have been the way I wanted to see it come, but this was how God gave it to us.... I asked one boy, who was on the floor, "What's happening to you right now?" He said "It's like electricity. I can't move." I was amazed by the effect of God's power on the human body. I suppose I thought that it would all be an inward work, such as conviction or repentance. I never imagined there would be strong physical manifestations.

But John wasn't as happy as I. He had never seen large numbers of people sprawled out over the floor.... He spent that night reading Scripture and historical accounts of revival from the lives of people like Whitefield and Wesley. . . . But his study did not yield conclusive answers to questions raised from the previous evening's events. By 5 A.M. John was desperate. He cried out to God, "Lord, if this is you, please tell me." A moment later the phone rang and a pastor friend of ours from Denver, Colorado was on the line. "John," he said, "I'm sorry I'm calling so early, but I have something really strange to tell you. I don't know what it means, but God wants me to say, 'It's Me, John.'"[3]

Likewise, as God broke Pharaoh's back and reestablished his reign over Israel he said, "I am the God of Abraham, of Isaac, and of Jacob." In his power, in his signs and wonders, he said, "It's Me."

SEVEN

A Future and a Hope

IN THE EXODUS, AS WE HAVE SEEN, God is King and Israel is his vassal. Following the death of Moses, he conquers the land of Canaan through Joshua. The period of the judges now follows in which God exercises rule over his realm. The constant battle with unregenerate human nature and the surrounding pagan environment assures us that Eden has not been restored; dominion is still in the devil's hands. This means that Israel must live in conflict and hope, consistently orienting her faith toward the future.

Once God's people are settled in the land, they become unhappy with his rule and demand a human king instead. Therefore, God surrenders his direct reign over them. At the same time, in his wisdom he sets the stage for reestablishing it through his messianic King. We turn now to this unfolding drama which concludes on an angel-filled night among shepherds in Bethlehem.

Yahweh Fights for Israel

Through his mighty judgments God invades Canaan, driving out Israel's enemies before her (see Exodus 34:10-11). At the Jordan River Joshua, God's "charismatic leader"[1] and Moses' successor, commands the people, "Consecrate yourselves, for tomorrow the LORD will do wonders among you" (Jos 3:5). The waters are then parted and, as in the Exodus, Israel enters the land walking on dry ground (Jos 3:17). Proper preparations are now made for the battles ahead. They include the circumcision of the new generation born in the wilderness and the celebration of the Passover meal. In an awesome revelation, similar to the burning bush, Joshua encounters an angel who identifies himself as the "captain of the host of the LORD" (Jos 5:14). Through this visitation, Yahweh shows that he will personally lead his troops, fighting Israel's battles to take possession of the land with his signs and wonders. Joshua now submits, and God's people are ready to march.

With Yahweh in command, the conquest begins with the siege of Jericho. The army, however, is reduced to parading around the city in battle dress. Without human help Yahweh collapses the walls and Israel mops up the defenseless population (Jos 6:20-21). Here is a clear sign that the God who conquered Egypt will also conquer Canaan. Other cities fall by more traditional tactics. It is Yahweh who draws the battle plans (Jos 8:2) and who controls the strategy (Jos 8:18). Moreover, he slays the Amorites with large hailstones (Jos 10:11) and stops the sun at Gibeon to facilitate the enemy's slaughter (Jos 10:13). And why is this? "For the LORD fought for Israel" (Jos 10:14, see 10:25, 42; 11:6, 8; 23:10). God's people sweep Canaan, dividing the land among their tribes (Jos 13:7).

In the final dramatic moment of his life, Joshua gathers Israel at Shechem. He renews the Mosaic covenant following the Hittite vassal treaty form. First, he reminds the people of God's mighty works. Next, he calls upon them to renounce the gods which their fathers "served beyond the River [Euphrates] and in Egypt" (Jos 24:14). This renunciation means that God will define Israel's reality as she subjects herself to him. Joshua, then, signs the covenant, "But as for me and my house, we will serve the LORD" (Jos 24:15), and the people follow, crying, "Far be it from us that we should forsake the LORD ... who did these great signs in our sight and preserved us.... We also will serve the LORD, for He is our God" (Jos 24:16-18).

Initial successes, however, fail to clear the land of hostile peoples, forcing Israel to live at war. As in Egypt, her battles are not only against flesh and blood but against the demon-powered idols surrounding her. As we saw in chapter four, the pagan nations always stand as a lethal threat to Israel's purity. Since treaties with them include treaties with their deities, accommodation to them is always an ugly reality. Furthermore, racial intermarriage means religious intermarriage, bringing with it the infection of idolatry (see Joshua 23:12-13). This explains why God's "holy wars" call for the annihilation of whole populations. Yahweh exercises his judgment upon the idolaters and protects his people from spiritual adultery. He is a jealous lover.

By giving Canaan to Israel, God proves himself faithful to his unconditional "royal grant" given to Abraham. Since he is the King who provides bountifully for his vassal, Israel will enjoy cities which she did not build and vineyards which she did not plant (Dt 6:10-11). At the same time, God promises to defend her against external threats by raising up charismatic leaders in times of national emergency. To this we now turn.

The Judges: Charismatic Leaders

The period of the Judges follows a predictable cycle, not as the result of some artificial "theology of history" made up by an ancient writer, but as the result of God's character and Israel's behavior. We must remember that God established his conditional covenant on Sinai and that covenant will be enforced. After a time of peace in the land, Israel goes into decline. Similar to the next generation after a great revival, the children of the conquest are ignorant of their parents' experience of God's mighty deeds. As the Book of Judges reports, "There arose another generation after [Joshua] . . . who did not know the LORD, nor yet the work which He had done for Israel" (Jgs 2:10). As a result, God's people intermarried with pagans and served their gods (Jgs 3:6). The verb "served" is to be taken literally; they renounced their exclusive allegiance to God and subjected themselves to the fertility gods of the land. As Judges recounts, "[They] forgot the LORD their God, and served the Baals and the Asheroth" (Jgs 3:7). This spiritual compromise and confusion leads to Yahweh's judgment. Because Israel is now a nation with a land, that judgment comes through enemy invasion.

Under impending threat, the people turn from their sin, crying out for mercy. God graciously responds by raising up leaders to rally Israel. These leaders are charismatic, that is, like Moses and Joshua, they are naturally gifted warriors who are anointed by the Spirit of God. For example, when Othniel was called, "The Spirit of the LORD came upon him, and He judged Israel" (Jgs 3:10). Furthermore, the judges triumph by divine power, showing that the battle is Yahweh's.[2] Thus, after Gideon complains, "Where are all . . . [Yahweh's] miracles which our fathers told us about?" (Jgs 6:13), God answers by producing one. He first requires Gideon to reduce his troops to almost nothing. Rather than wielding the sword, the remaining handful frightens the enemy, causing panic in their camp. In the darkness and confusion they end up slaughtering themselves (Jgs 7:22). Now, no one will doubt that it is God who gets Israel victory and who receives the glory. This miracle is thrown in her face!

After their enemies are defeated, God's people normally enjoy an extended period of peace. With the blessing of their sovereign King upon them, they walk in his ways and receive the fruit of the land. As we have seen, peace often breeds indolence and sin. At this point, the cycle of judgment, repentance, the cry for help, and the raising up of another charismatic leader begins again.

The advantages of the period of the judges are many. God alone is King in Israel.[3] He maintains direct authority over his people by not institutionalizing his rule in a human king. Thus, they are forced to retain their immediate dependence upon him. Moreover, he is free to provide the judges whom he desires, credentialed only by him. In this, he proves himself to be the living God in Israel's midst. Unlike the dumb idols, he speaks, calls, leads, wins battles, and blesses the land. For example, he regularly dispatches "the angel of the LORD" from his heavenly court to bring messages of judgment and hope to his people (Jgs 2:1; 5:23; 6:11; 13:3). Moreover, the Spirit of God is alive and active. As the Spirit comes upon the judges, we know that the mighty King is not aloof in heaven. While he reigns there, he is also imminent among his people, powerfully at work. Thus, the pretensions and burdens of a human monarchy are unknown, and God alone is glorified.

This is theocracy. God himself provides Israel with worship, prosperity, order, and security. Since she is dependent upon him for everything, she is responsible to worship him alone. Moreover, since he both creates and controls nature, he provides for her livelihood. He also establishes her moral order, instituting the application and execution of the law by the judges. As Commander in Chief of Israel's armies, God calls up his leaders and provides for her protection. She is secure in him alone.

What, then, is Israel's response to God as King? As we have seen, her first response is worship. This takes place at the tabernacle and at local shrines. Her second response is obedience. Here, however, Israel's weakness is the weakness of sinful, fallen human nature. Since she was to be God's servant and live in his kingdom, everyone should have done what was right in God's eyes. Nevertheless, at the close of the Book of Judges, we read, "In those days there was no king in Israel; everyone did what was right in his own eyes" (Jgs 21:25). This sorry conclusion prepares us for the creation of the monarchy.

King of Kings

With the anointing of Saul as king, a fundamental dilemma is now posed: How can God still be King and, at the same time, create a human king who will compete with him? Since Israel knows that Yahweh rules, the demand for a human king means apostasy. But much to our surprise, God grants this request and calls Saul, blessing him with his Spirit. But who really reigns, Yahweh or Saul? And how can this dilemma be resolved? Let us turn to the history of the monarchy for our answers.

Samuel, the final judge, brings the era of God's direct reign in Israel to its end. As the political landscape changes with the revival of the great pagan empires, the elders of the people come to him at Ramah demanding a king "to judge us like all the nations" (1 Sm 8:5). Weary of depending upon God for their leadership, they want a stability and an order which they can see. Moreover, they want the benefits of royalty; centralized authority, tradition, and a standing army with which to dominate their buffer states. Brokenhearted, Samuel turns to Yahweh and hears this fateful word: "Listen to the voice of the people in regard to all that they say to you, for they have not rejected you, but they have rejected Me from being king over them" (1 Sm 8:7). This becomes a decisive turning point for Israel. From now on the crucial question stands: When will God resume his rightful, direct reign over his people again?

The fact that God is King creates a deep ambivalence towards human kingship throughout the Old Testament. Since the people have rejected Yahweh's rule, the monarchy is his accommodation to their rebellion. When the kings oppress her and the people cry to Yahweh, Samuel warns, "the LORD will not answer you in that day" (1 Sm 8:18). Thus, in God's "passive wrath," the signs and wonders of His kingdom die out.[4] It is this rather than some dispensational theory of history which accounts for the decline of the miraculous in Israel. After a brief charismatic period during Saul's and David's reigns, Israel cannot expect God's direct intervention against invading armies. In fact, he will use the pagan nations to bring the fire of his judgment upon faithless Israel instead (see Psalm 106:34-43).

Nevertheless, it is God who establishes the monarchy.

Therefore, the king represents God's rule among his people. God grants him a special relationship with himself: God will be like a father to him and he will be like a son (compare Psalm 2). From the vantage point of the New Testament, we see that this relationship is modeled on God's relationship with his Son in heaven. Thus, by establishing the monarchy, God not only accommodates himself to Israel's sin, but also provides the instrument by which he will fulfill his kingdom purpose. This centers, as we shall see, in his covenant with David which holds the promise of the coming Messiah.

Accepting the people's demand, God now instructs Samuel to anoint Saul as Israel's first king. After this the Spirit of God comes mightily upon him and he prophesies (1 Sm 10:10). Later, when Israel accepts his reign at Gilgal (1 Sm 11:15), Samuel, in accord with the ambivalence toward the monarchy which we have noted, presents a double message: you rejected God as King; he has chosen Saul as king. That Israel has sinned is made clear when Samuel calls upon Yahweh to destroy the wheat harvest at the moment of Saul's ascent to the throne: "So Samuel called to the LORD, and the LORD sent thunder and rain that day; and all the people greatly feared the LORD and Samuel" (1 Sm 12:18).[5] Their moment of joy is now made bitter.

There is a lesson for us to learn here. God may give us what we demand, accommodating himself to our sin. There is a cost, however, and the cost of the monarchy for Israel was generations of turmoil and then final destruction as a nation. When all her cards were finally played, God took back the game. He lets us get to the end of ourselves, however long the process, and then steps in again: "Lord of all or not Lord at all."

Accepting his new calling as king, Saul leads Israel in battle and she rallys behind him. However, he sins presumptuously by sacrificing before God (1 Sm 13:8-14). God, therefore, rejects Saul and sends Samuel to anoint David as his heir. As a supernatural sign of this appointment and as the means of its execution, the Spirit of God now falls upon David (1 Sm

16:13). At the same time the Spirit departs from Saul and is replaced by "an evil spirit from the LORD [which] terrorized him" (1 Sm 16:14).

After Saul's battlefield death, David is proclaimed king. Since God's anointing is upon him, Saul's heirs fail to establish their dynastic succession. David then secures the kingdom, eventually uniting all the tribes under his rule at Hebron (2 Sm 5:3). Moreover, he continues to defeat his enemies through Yahweh who provides his battle plans (2 Sm 5:23-24). In this context God makes a covenant with David promising to make his name great, establish Israel in the land in peace, and build a house (dynasty) for him (2 Sm 7:9-11). This final promise becomes the instrument of Israel's messianic hope.

This covenant with David is similar to the covenant with Abraham, modeled on the Hittite "royal grant"—unconditional and gracious in its promise. Thus, God says,

> "I will establish the throne of [your son's] kingdom forever. I will be a father to him and he will be a son to Me; ... And your house and your kingdom shall endure before Me forever; your throne shall be established forever." (2 Sm 7:13-16)

Here, again, we are faced with an apparent contradiction: either God will reign or David's son will reign; either there will be a divine King or a human king over Israel. What appears to be contradiction in the Old Testament, however, is resolved in the New Testament. Thus, it is Jesus Christ, the eternal Son of the Father who will restore God's direct reign over his people. At the same time, by wedding his deity to our humanity, he will fulfill the covenant promise made to David to have an heir on his throne forever. In Jesus, God's rule will be both direct and delegated and his kingdom will come again to his people.

David's life reflects the heights and depths of Israel's relationship with God. As a man after God's own heart, David becomes the archetype of the Messiah, establishing a glorious kingdom for God's people. At the same time, (to paraphrase Luther) David both believes boldly and sins boldly. Thus, after his affair with Bathsheba, a downward spiral of adultery, deception, and murder unfolds which almost costs him his throne. Moreover, with the death of Bathsheba's illicit child, civil war wrenches Israel in two. While David survives this catastrophe, his reign is never again the same. His bright star now fades from view. Israel's hope cannot be fulfilled by an earthly king. Salvation from her enemies and the restoration of God's rule lies in the future. It is God's to promise and it is God's to perform.

Hope for Tomorrow

With a few rare exceptions (such as King Josiah), the history of Israel under her kings is troubled and tragic. After the glory of Solomon's reign which includes building the temple in Jerusalem, the kingdom divides. The northern tribes endanger the pure faith of God by accommodating themselves to their pagan environment (see 2 Kings 17:7-18). Judah in the south fares little better. In the dynastic struggles which follow, it is clear that the anointing given by Yahweh to Saul and David is not automatically inherited.

Fortunately, God's power is not absent. That which is withheld from the kings is now given to the prophets. Thus these uncredentialed "charismatics," such as Elijah and Elisha, speak his word and do his works, performing his signs and wonders. Elijah, not the king, calls down fire from heaven against the prophets of Baal (1 Kgs 18:38). This does not, as many modern theologians hold, signify that a new period of revelation has begun, since prophecy has been God's gift to Israel since the time of Moses. Rather it signifies that the direct rule of Yahweh is now being exercised outside the institution of the monarchy. Moreover, it is the lay prophets who have access into God's heavenly court (for example, Micaiah, 1 Kgs 22:19-23). Like Moses, they receive a direct word from him and bring that word to Israel. The sign that they speak the truth is that their word works; it is fulfilled in its time (compare Deuteronomy 18:22).

Since the monarchy now stands under judgment, the signs and wonders of the past become a distant memory to "official Israel." Like the anointing of the Spirit, they too cannot be institutionally guaranteed by a human king; they are Yahweh's alone to perform. God's silence toward the monarchy exhibits his "passive wrath." He removes himself from the idolatry and immorality perpetuated by foreign alliances and foreign wives. At the same time, in his "active wrath," after giving clear prophetic warnings, God destroys the northern kingdom with the fall of Samaria in 721 B.C. and the southern kingdom with the fall of Jerusalem in 586 B.C. In these events Assyria and Babylon become the instruments of his judgment against his own people (see Isaiah 10:5). In fact, it is they, not Israel, who manifest his kingdom. Even Cyrus the Persian will later be called God's anointed (Is 45:1). Nevertheless, in the midst of decay, rebellion, and sin, hope for Israel's restoration burns even more brightly. God's messengers, the prophets, not only bring words of punishment, they also bring words of promise. God has not abandoned his people. The blessing of Abraham for Israel and the nations will be fulfilled.

Moreover, throughout this period, the temple liturgy and popular piety represented in the psalms portray the continuing expectation of God's intervention. The glowing memory of the signs and wonders in the Exodus sustains hope that Yahweh will intervene again, if not for the whole nation, then at least for the pious remnant (Ps 105:27; 106:7). These interventions include deliverance from illness (Ps 6), enemies (Ps 5:8-10), and death itself (Ps 16:10-11; 23:6). If God were not the living God and if he did not answer prayer, then psalms such as these could not have retained their relevance in the life of God's people.

Through the prophets' words and works and the peoples' prayers the fire of faith in God the King burns brightly.

Disappointment over the monarchy serves to keep Israel's gaze on the distant horizon, in the hope that God would do a new work again and reestablish his rightful reign in her midst.

In all of this there is a warning. If we presume to inherit God's anointing by tradition or ritual we are either misled or foolish. The history of Israel and the history of the church both disprove this. If we allow institutions to control God's work rather than become the instruments of that work, we will experience his silence in judgment and the absence of his miraculous interventions. Like the period of the monarchy, signs and wonders will be withdrawn. If we so organize our churches that we disenfranchise charismatic leadership when God brings it to us, then we become apostate from his kingdom and usurp his rightful rule in our midst. God will continue to be God. He will raise up other leaders and other movements and leave us as the dead to bury the dead. Like Israel, however, beyond the ashes of our unbelief stands the shining promise of God and that promise will be fulfilled.

The Promise

The prophets proclaim that God will reestablish his direct reign throughout Israel. As Isaiah says, "Behold, the Lord God will come with might, With His arm ruling for Him" (Is 40:10). This coming will usher in the "day of the LORD" which will mean judgment for his enemies (Am 5:18-20), evil powers, their idols (Is 2:18-20), and the nations who serve them. It will also mean salvation for his elect (Mal 4:1-3). God alone will be King in that day. As he says through Ezekiel, "As I live, . . . surely with a mighty hand and with an outstretched arm and with wrath poured out, I shall be king over you" (Ez 20:33).

At the same time, this reign is to be exercised by God's messianic King. Thus, it is both direct and delegated. The human child born to sit on David's throne is also God, bearing the divine names, "Mighty God, Eternal Father" (Is 9:6). Likewise, the psalmist declares that the anointed King on

Mount Zion who rules the nations is the Son of God (Ps 2:2-7).

In light of our study, it is no surprise that the coming of the Messiah will usher in God's reign. All the benefits of kingship —worship, order, prosperity, and security—will be fulfilled.

First, God's people "will be called the priests of the Lord" (Is 61:6). Their worship will have a renewed temple at its center (Ez 40-48). Second, there is order with the law no longer imposed upon us as an external demand, but written upon our hearts through the New Covenant (Jer 31:31). Third, there is prosperity as the land becomes fruitful again (Ps 72). Fourth, there is security and lasting peace as the Warrior-King destroys the demon idols, returns Israel from exile with joy (Is 61:7), and the nations beat their swords into plowshares and study war no more (Is 2:4). A new Eden will then emerge as the lion lies down with the lamb, ending the travail of earth (Is 11:6-8). All of this will be accomplished as God's Spirit is poured out upon all flesh (Jl 2:28) and all of God's people become charismatic leaders (Nm 11:29).

God's unconditional love is not for Israel alone. Abraham's call was for the blessing of the nations and they too will share in the age of salvation (Is 2:2-3). Once again his kingdom will be fully manifest upon this planet. His rejected reign will be restored. Is this bright hope merely the mythological thinking of a primitive nation? To answer this question let us turn to the New Testament. It opens with angels on a star-filled night singing of God's glory and proclaiming peace on earth. In Bethlehem, God's salvation breaks into history once again.

EIGHT

The Kingdom Come: The Ministry of Jesus

THE NEW TESTAMENT RESOUNDS WITH FULFILLMENT, documenting that God's reign has now broken in upon us. Again and again in the Gospels we read: "...that the Scriptures might be fulfilled." Here the writers evidence a clear sense of continuity between what is promised in the Old Testament and what is now taking place, and it is only our anti-supernatural bias which makes us stumble over this. For past generations, the fact of fulfillment was a telling argument for the truthfulness of the gospel message and the inspiration of its authors.

All of the Old Testament expectations concerning the coming of God's kingdom are addressed in the New Testament. First century Israel lived in high anticipation that Yahweh's apocalyptic reign would defeat the devil, send Rome packing, and restore our dominion in Eden. Seated on David's throne, the Messiah would usher in all of this, fulfilling the covenant promise made so long ago.

No wonder, then, that Jesus' announcement, "The time is fulfilled, and the kingdom of God is at hand" (Mk 1:15), stirred such enthusiasm and controversy. What did he mean when he heralded the kingdom? The answer to this question has preoccupied generations of scholars. Not even the radical

New Testament critic Rudolf Bultmann would doubt that this was the center of his proclamation. He writes, "The dominant concept of Jesus' message is the *Reign of God*. Jesus proclaims its immediately impending eruption, now already making itself felt."[1] But what did Jesus mean?

The Kingdom Come and Coming

Albert Schweitzer advanced the first possibility. In his classic, *The Quest of the Historical Jesus*, he rightly insists that Jesus' message and ministry must be understood in the context of first century Jewish apocalyptic thought. Basing his research, then, upon this presupposition, Schweitzer proposes that Jesus did believe himself to be the Messiah-elect and that he ministered in the expectation that he would see the final, supernatural arrival of the kingdom in his lifetime. Thus, according to Schweitzer, he hoped for its future in breaking which would end history as we know it, and he determined to bring it about. This explains the enigmatic verse where, as Jesus sends out the Twelve to preach the kingdom, he promises that they will not have passed through all the cities of Israel before the end comes (Mt 10:23). With the urgency of a theological dogmatism, he expected to command history and the future itself. He was, however, disappointed. The disciples returned from their mission and all was quiet. This led Jesus to take the drastic action of going to Jerusalem in order to force God's hand. Assuming that there had to be a time of suffering, the so-called messianic birth pangs, before the kingdom would break in, he determined to be rejected and by this, pave the way for its coming. He was again deluded. As Jesus threw himself on the wheel of history, he was crushed by it. In his failure, apocalyptic thought itself was destroyed, leaving us with the noble ideal of Jesus and the radical nature of his ethics. It is hard not to conclude from this that our Lord was merely another misled Jewish fanatic.[2]

The second possibility is offered by C.H. Dodd, Professor of

New Testament at Cambridge, in his answer to Schweitzer.³ For Dodd, Jesus was not a misled Jewish fanatic trying to force the future kingdom but the real Messiah of Israel bringing in the present kingdom. Thus, when Jesus announced that the kingdom of God is at hand, he meant that it is here now, teaching a "realized eschatology." For example, many of Jesus' parables show that the kingdom is here, working, even as a "grain of mustard seed." Rather than being an otherworldly fanatic, Jesus really did usher in the kingdom which is centered in God's forgiving love for his children. If Schweitzer was right that the ministry of Jesus must be understood in the context of Jewish apocalyptic thought, then Dodd was also right in asserting that in Jesus the kingdom is not just a future event but a present reality.

The third possibility is that Jesus proclaimed a kingdom which is future and present at the same time. Here we are on dead center. Jesus believed in the reestablishment of God's rightful reign in Israel and among the Gentile nations. He believed his mission to be the inauguration of that reign. While God's kingdom was present in his ministry, however, it was not fully present. There would still be a future fulfillment when Satan, sin, and death would be completely destroyed. At the same time, Jesus had come to manifest God's direct rule here and to defeat our enemies. This means that the future messianic kingdom has dawned; it has broken in upon us. Furthermore, it is God's plan to spread this kingdom around the world and down through history until its consummation. We can sum up the thought in this way: the kingdom is really here but it is not fully here. Believers, then, live in a kingdom come and coming.

The structure of New Testament thought is that history is determined by two ages: this present evil age and the coming messianic age. Oscar Cullmann in his book *Christ and Time* shows us that this structure is not optional for understanding and retaining the biblical message. Illustrating the meaning of Jesus' coming, Cullmann uses the classic example of the World War II distinction between "D" Day and "V" Day. When the allies established their beachhead at Normandy on "D" Day, the war in Europe was really won. At the same time, "V" Day, Victory Day, still stood before them and the battle went on. Likewise, when Jesus came to earth as God's Messiah (Deliverer), it was "D" Day, the beachhead of God's kingdom was secured. It literally broke in upon us as the future became present. Nevertheless, we still await its final consummation. When Jesus returns it will be "V" Day.[4] The Christian life is then lived in this tension.

The reason why this truth is so gripping is that it illumines so much of our present experience. It explains both our sense of triumph in Christ and the continuing spiritual warfare which we fight on many fronts. It explains the reality that we have died with Christ and, at the same time, that the flesh still wars against the spirit. It explains why people are dramatically healed today by the power of God and also continue to get sick and die. It explains why we have strength through weakness and life through death. If we break the tension we either end up in perfectionism, on the one hand, or despair, on the other. The good news is that the future kingdom is now at work in the present and that we are enabled to live between the times.

The Supernatural Revisited

As we read the Gospels, it is clear that God is on the move. The supernatural has become the expected as his heavenly kingdom is open to us once again. For example, as in the times of the patriarchs and the Exodus, angels now frequently appear bearing his messages. Thus, Gabriel comes to the temple in order to inform the priest Zacharias of the birth of his son John. Later, Gabriel bears a similar word to the virgin Mary, telling her that she will be the entry point for the incarnation. Next, an angel tells Mary's fiance, Joseph, that she is pregnant by the Holy Spirit. Angels announce Jesus' birth to the shepherds and guide Joseph to flee from Herod's wrath. They later minister to Jesus in times of stress, herald his resurrection, and prophesy his glorious return. These supernatural messengers, so visible when God gave his "royal grant" to Abraham, have now returned in force.

God's Spirit is also supernaturally at work. The rabbis taught that the Spirit had been taken from Israel due to her sin but would return when the Messiah came. No wonder the New Testament is filled with his presence. Thus, it is the Spirit who miraculously conceives Jesus in Mary's womb. And, the Spirit descends upon Jesus at his baptism, anointing him for his messianic ministry. Throughout his public career Jesus ministers through the power and the gifts of the Spirit. His supernatural wisdom, healings, and miracles come through the Spirit's presence. Later, he promises this same gift to his disciples and to us as well.

Furthermore, God raises up prophets. His voice, so long silent, is heard once again in the land. For example, Luke's Gospel begins with Zacharias, John the Baptist's father, uttering an extensive prophecy concerning his son's future. Then the prophet Simeon and the prophetess Anna appear in the temple to bless and welcome the Messiah. Later, John the Baptist boldly prophesies the Messiah's coming, preparing the people to receive him. Jesus is also seen as a prophetic messenger announcing God's salvation and calling his people to repentance.

Supremely, God himself speaks directly from heaven. He calls Jesus his "Beloved Son" when he is baptized by John in the Jordan and later repeats this on the Mount of Transfiguration.

It is worth noting that these supernatural manifestations of God's kingdom also provoke their satanic equivalent. Once the Son of God enters our history, there is a counterattack from the kingdom of darkness. The devil now stalks Jesus, tempting him directly to abandon his messianic mission. Later, the demons cry out in his presence, identifying him as the Son of God. When Peter tempts the Lord not to fulfill his destiny in

Jerusalem. Jesus sees Satan's shadow lurking behind his naiveté. The climax comes when the devil actually enters Judas who then goes out to destroy Jesus.

What this tells us is that the context for the kingdom is the intervention of the supernatural. Heaven is open and judgment, God's silent, "passive wrath," is lifted. Once again his reign is revealed, and once again, the devil fights back. This is the proper setting for Jesus' announcement that the kingdom of God is at hand, and if the kingdom really is here, this must also be the proper setting for our hearing this announcement today. It is no surprise that signs and wonders don't merely prove revelation. They *are* revelation, and where we are being renewed, such manifestations will become a part of our current expectation and experience.

The Kingdom Is at Hand

In the opening of his Gospel, Mark tells us that after John the Baptist was imprisoned, Jesus entered Galilee proclaiming, "The time is fulfilled, and the kingdom of God is at hand; repent and believe in the gospel" (Mk 1:15). This is the heart of Jesus' message. The synoptic authors (Matthew, Mark, and Luke) unanimously confirm this. When they summarize Jesus' preaching it is the kingdom at hand (see Matthew 4:23; Luke 4:43). Moreover, when they summarize the preaching of the disciples it is the same (Mt 10:7). What does it mean for the kingdom of God to be "at hand?"

First of all, for Jesus the time of fulfillment has dawned. In the context of the Old Testament, this means that God's covenant promise, blessing Israel and the nations through his "royal grant" to Abraham, is here. No wonder Jesus promises, "And I say to you, that many shall come from east and west, and recline at table with Abraham, and Isaac, and Jacob, in the kingdom of heaven" (Mt 8:11). At the same time, the further "royal grant" given to David, the promise of an heir seated upon his throne forever, is also here. As the angel Gabriel tells

Mary, "And behold, you will conceive in your womb, and bear a son, and you shall name him Jesus. He will be great, and will be called the Son of the Most High; and the Lord God will give Him the throne of His father David; and He will reign over the house of Jacob forever; and His kingdom will have no end" (Lk 1:31-33). In sum, God's unconditional gifts, his salvation and his reign, have arrived in Jesus.

Second, Jesus sees this fulfillment centered in the "kingdom of God." The kingdom, as we have seen, is the reign of God over his realm, establishing his authority over his people as they submit to him in worship. All other allegiances are broken, all other authorities are surrendered. Where God reigns, his justice and his blessings come upon his people. Moreover, all his enemies must flee. Jesus, then, announces that this kingdom is "at hand." While some have taken the phrase "at hand" to mean that the kingdom is near or close, I believe that we should take it spatially, that is, the kingdom is within reach. In other words, Jesus proclaims that the King is here and if you reach out and touch him you will touch the kingdom. For this reason he tells the Pharisees not to look for the signs of its coming: "For behold, the kingdom of God is in your midst" (Lk 17:21).

After Mark summarizes Jesus' message of the kingdom, he immediately documents its presence by telling stories about the ministry of the King. Through the mighty works of Jesus, his signs and wonders, we see that the kingdom is indeed within reach and our broken humanity is being restored to God's original order. This is the decisive turning point of all history.

We have already noted that Jesus' proclamation of God's kingdom sent a shock throughout Israel. But it was not simply the message of Jesus that kindled such hope. After all, Matthew tells us that this message was also shared by John the Baptist (Mt 3:2). It was the *ministry* of Jesus that drew the crowds and shook the foundations of Jewish religion, for in that ministry the kingdom of God was present. Theologians today note that where the kingdom is being manifested, creation is being healed. Thus, as Jesus heals the sick, casts out demons, and raises the dead, God's reign and order is revealed.

It is essential to realize that the kingdom became a "lower storey," earthly reality through the miraculous work of Jesus. By these works he justified his messianic ministry to the skeptical messengers from John the Baptist (Lk 7:18-23). By these works he also actually did the work of the King, redeeming his subjects from sin, sickness, and Satan and restoring them to the heavenly rule of the sovereign God.

I remember hearing Francis MacNutt ask the question, "If you wanted to start a worldwide movement what would you do?" He then suggested that our modern methods would demand recruiting a bright, ambitious staff, engaging in comprehensive market research, and setting up major media campaigns nursed by wide fundraising efforts. Following these preparations, the movement would then be launched by the direct power centers of political influence. Jesus' method, however, was much simpler. He just healed a few people, and as he did this news spread like wildfire. Multitudes engulfed him, eager to hear his teaching and see his works. As he ministered, Jesus may not have attracted the aristocratic elite, but the sick were certainly there. They knew their need and when the Great Physician came to town, they turned out in force.

Luke documents the simple but powerful beginning of Jesus' public ministry. Invited to teach in the synagogue at Nazareth, he is handed the Isaiah scroll and reads the text from the opening of chapter 61:

> The Spirit of the Lord is upon Me,
> Because He anointed Me to preach the gospel to the poor.
> He has sent Me to proclaim release to the captives,
> And recovery of sight to the blind,
> To set free those who are downtrodden,
> To proclaim the favorable year of the Lord. (Lk 4:17-19)

Then, assuming the authoritative, rabbinic position of teaching by sitting, Jesus announces, "Today this Scripture has been fulfilled in your hearing" (Lk 4:21). Here is Jesus' agenda for ministry. What does it entail?

First of all, Jesus has experienced the anointing of God's Spirit for his mission. Certainly he was never without the Spirit. Nevertheless, when he was baptized by John the Spirit came upon him in power (Lk 3:21-22). This anointing was similar to that received by Moses, the judges, and Saul and David when they were made kings over Israel. Jesus is the culmination of God's charismatic leaders. While this anointing meant that he spoke with authority, it also meant that he ministered in power.[5] Luke reports, "And Jesus returned to Galilee in the power of the Spirit" (Lk 4:14); "For power was coming from Him and healing them all" (Lk 6:19). Later, Jesus promises the same anointing to his disciples before they begin their ministry (Acts 1:8). They too will lead the church by the same charisma.

Second, Jesus came to preach good news to the poor, the spiritually dispossessed of the land. He came to evangelize the lost. Not only does he preach to the multitudes, he also eats with publicans (tax collectors) and sinners (Lk 5:30) and welcomes the tears of a prostitute. He brings those who believe to the authentic worship of God, and then pours down the bounty of his kingdom in forgiveness, healing, and material blessing, represented, for example, by his feeding the five thousand.

Third, Jesus came to preach "release to the captives," namely to set free the demonized. No wonder Luke follows this sermon by showing Jesus casting out a demon in the synagogue at Capernaum (Lk 4:31-37). Thus, Mark sums up Jesus' ministry: "And He went into their synagogues throughout all Galilee, preaching and casting out the demons" (Mk 1:39). Here are authentic "power encounters" as Jesus invades the devil's domain, reclaiming God's creation as the triumphant Warrior-King.

Fourth, Jesus offers "recovery of sight to the blind." Since he literally heals blind people, this should not be taken metaphorically (Lk 7:21). His ministry restores the fallen creation to its original wholeness. Where the kingdom comes, lepers are cleansed, disease is healed, the lame walk, and even the dead are raised. In these signs and wonders God makes his kingdom real.

Fifth, Jesus came as the Warrior-King to free the downtrodden, to liberate all those in bondage, economically, politically, socially, or religiously, and who are controlled by the evil principalities and powers. For this reason He consistently violates the regulations of Jewish tradition (see Mark 7:1-13) which have dehumanized God's people and brought them into bondage. He announces the "favorable year of the Lord," the Jubilee year representing salvation or "release" (see Leviticus 25:10).

The lengthy accounts of Jesus' miracles, his signs and wonders, provide the exegesis for this synagogue text. Thus, they do not prove his deity, they prove that the kingdom is here. God's reign is now aggressively operating through Jesus, reclaiming his lost kingdom from the enemy who has been bound and whose house is now being plundered (Mk 3:27). Thus, Jesus demonstrates to John the Baptist that he is the Messiah, God's anointed King, by what he does (Lk 7:22).

The message of the kingdom without the ministry of the kingdom, the word without the work, would make Jesus either an idealist or a gnostic or a myth. Despite our anti-supernatural bias, we do not have the luxury of separating the miracles from the message; they stand or fall together. Throughout the entire Bible, God's kingdom operates directly and dynamically. Israel could not have been redeemed from Egypt apart from God's mighty acts of war. She could not have been sustained in the wilderness apart from God's heavenly provision, and she could not have conquered the Promised Land apart from his battle plans. How then can we deny the mighty acts of Jesus when he enters our history as the King in person to reclaim God's creation from the devil?

The Message of Jesus

What then is the nature of this kingdom established in the ministry of Jesus? As we have learned from our previous study, the reign of God, his kingship, determines Jesus' teaching and will determine our answer.

First, God establishes his kingdom in order to create the proper *worship* of himself. This is clearly on Jesus' heart as he zealously cleanses the temple. No wonder he answers the question about the greatest commandment by citing Deuteronomy 6:4, "Hear, O Israel; The Lord our God is one Lord; and you shall love the Lord your God with all your heart, and with all your soul, and with all your mind, and with all your strength" (Mk 12:29-30). When an inquiring scribe agrees with him, he adds, "You are not far from the kingdom of God" (Mk 12:34). But what is true worship? In a word, it is submission. Again and again, Jesus calls his hearers to come into the kingdom by surrendering themselves to God's reign (Mt 7:21, see Matthew 5:20; 18:3).

Since worship as surrender includes stripping ourselves before God, Jesus tells us that the kingdom of heaven is like a treasure hidden in a field, for which a man sells everything in order to possess it (Mt 13:44). Or it is like a costly pearl, for which a merchant sells all that he has in order to buy it (Mt 13:45-46). This surrender also often includes being broken by God; in our adult arrogance we must become as a child in order to enter the kingdom. As Jesus solemnly warns, "Truly I say to you, whoever does not receive the kingdom of God like a child shall not enter it at all" (Mk 10:15). Moreover, the content of this childlike attitude consists of repentance and humility: "Truly I say to you, unless you are converted and become like children, you shall not enter the kingdom of heaven. Whoever then humbles himself as this child, he is the greatest in the kingdom of heaven" (Mt 18:3-4).

This demand for humility explains why it is so hard for a wealthy man to enter the kingdom since his standing and security are found in his possessions (Mt 19:23-24). Thus, it is only through a radical transformation, being born again, that we can see the kingdom of God (Jn 3:3). This is symbolized by Jesus' call to discipleship which includes self-denial, taking up the cross and following him (Mk 8:34).[6] Here is his frontal assault on the pride which expelled Satan from heaven and which sent Adam and Eve packing from the garden. To bow before Jesus in worship means to surrender all that we are and have.

Second, along with heartfelt worship, Jesus reestablishes God's moral *order* for our lives. Thus, he calls us to seek first the kingdom of God "*and His righteousness*" (Mt 6:33, italics mine) and teaches us to pray, "Thy kingdom come. Thy will be done, On earth . . ." (Mt 6:10). Jesus' demand for righteousness is more than mere external obedience, so he tells his disciples, "Unless your righteousness surpasses that of the scribes and Pharisees, you shall not enter the kingdom of heaven" (Mt 5:20). For this reason he is as concerned with our motives as he is with our behavior. Before God, anger is as great a sin as murder, and lust is as great a sin as adultery (Mt 5:21-32). The radical nature of Jesus' demand for perfection in God's kingdom is such that "if your eye causes you to stumble, cast it out; it is better for you to enter the kingdom of God with one eye, than having two eyes, to be cast into hell" (Mk 9:47). Ultimately, Jesus' standard of judgment is taken from the very character of God: "Therefore you are to be perfect, as your heavenly Father is perfect" (Mt 5:48).

Our despair over this demand makes us ready for the gospel. By his perfect obedience, Jesus fulfills it for us, including all the laws of the Mosaic covenant, the vassal treaty. This clears the way for him to remove the curse of the law from us (the Righteous One dying for the unrighteous), so that we may receive the salvation-blessing of God (see Galatians 3:6-14).[7] Jesus is now the Mediator, standing between us and the law.[7] Thus, he fulfills the law *for us* and then he fulfills the law *in us* as he gives us his Spirit and leads us into a life of righteousness (see Romans 8:4).

As the bearer of God's kingdom, Jesus not only reestablishes, intensifies, and fulfills God's moral order, he also enforces that order. As he says in John's Gospel: "For not even the Father judges anyone, but He has given all judgment to the Son" (Jn 5:22). Thus, he warns: "For whoever is ashamed of Me and My words in this adulterous and sinful generation, the Son of Man will also be ashamed of him when He comes in the glory of His Father with the holy angels" (Mk 8:38).

What we do with Jesus now determines our eternal destiny. While friendship with him is his great gift to us, we need to combine this with a sense of awe before his majesty. As suggested in chapter one, he is much more than a "good guy," a modern Jesus who pals around with us, reassuring us that we are okay. He is our Lord and Judge.

Third, along with worship and order, Jesus provides *prosperity* for his people. He brings the free grace of God to us. He teaches that the kingdom of heaven is like a king who forgives his servant an enormous debt (Mt 18:23-35). Moreover, it is like a generous landowner who pays a day's wages to those who have worked little (Mt 20:1-15). While we are to be perfect as our heavenly Father is perfect, Jesus also commands us, "Be merciful, just as your Father is merciful" (Lk 6:36). Forgiveness is the currency of the kingdom.

Along with unlimited grace, Jesus presents the kingdom as a realm of great bounty. When the seeds of the kingdom are sown in the midst of adversity, they produce enormous fruitfulness (Mk 4:8, 20). Moreover, right now the kingdom is growing in the world (Mk 4:31-32). It is leaven, leavening the whole lump (Mt 13:33). For those who enter it there is a sumptuous banquet; they "recline at table" with Abraham, Isaac, and Jacob (Mt 8:11). Jesus brings "new wine"; his presence is like that of a bridegroom at a wedding (Lk 5:34-39). As I noted in chapter one, when I was filled with the Holy Spirit, this spiritual bounty became an experiential reality to me. The most remarkable part of the event was not my speaking in tongues but the explosion of joy in my heart.

The prosperity of those in the kingdom is eschatological. That is, we now live, as we have seen, in a kingdom come and coming. In this age we will experience the future, but we still await its complete fulfillment. On the one hand, we will know a measure of material blessing. As Jesus promises, when we seek first the Father's kingdom and his righteousness, then "all these things [food, drink, and clothing] shall be added to you" (Mt 6:33). God's bounty, however, comes in the midst of this fallen world. Thus, Jesus expresses the mix when he promises houses, brothers and sisters and mothers and children and farms for his disciples who have left all to follow him "along with persecutions; and in the world to come, eternal life" (Mk 10:29-30).

This mention of persecutions rightly throws the shadow of the cross over our lives. Joy and suffering are to be our lot in this age (Rom 5:1-5). As Jesus suffered, so will we suffer (Mt 10:24-25). He offers us no "prosperity gospel" of health, wealth, and happiness in this world (which could only be produced in materialistic America and has little relevance for most Christians who live in the Third World). By this he keeps our eyes looking toward the horizon for the eternal life yet to be revealed.

Fourth, along with worship, order, and prosperity, the King provides *security* for his people. When Jesus ushers in God's kingdom, the first thing that he does to defeat our enemies is exercise dominion over the devil and all of his works.[8] After overcoming temptation in the wilderness, he drives the demons out in order to reclaim God's good earth from the enemy. Thus, Jesus says, "But if I cast out demons by the Spirit of God, then the kingdom of God has come upon you" (Mt 12:28). Here the Warrior-King fights his real battles for us.

While Jesus' primary assault is on the devil, he also attacks the manifestations of his evil kingdom in the religious pride and burdensome regulations of the Pharisees (Mt 23:13-28). He charges them with being "hypocrites" (Mt 6:2), caring for their prideful places of honor rather than for the well-being of

God's people (Mt 23:6). They are "whitewashed tombs" (Mt 23:27), concerned for the style rather than the substance of their lives. Behind their presumption, Jesus sees the shadow of the evil one. Their converts are made children of hell (Mt 23:15).

Once Jesus has broken the power of the enemy and religious hypocrisy over us, he wraps us in his security, promising to protect us, giving us this assurance, "Do not be afraid, little flock, for your Father has chosen gladly to give you the kingdom" (Lk 12:32). This is our ultimate security.

Our Kingdom Prayer

These central themes of the kingdom—worship, order, prosperity, and security—are summed up by the so-called Lord's prayer. Most church people, as they mumble through it Sunday by Sunday, think that this prayer is about the fatherhood of God, the brotherhood of man, and being good. It is, in fact, a weapon of intercession for God's reign. As Jesus teaches us to pray, he first leads us into worship: "Our Father who art in heaven, Hallowed be Thy name." Addressing God as "Father," he leads us into intimacy with the mighty King which he himself enjoys as the only Son. Next, as we pray for God's name to be hallowed, or separated from all that is unholy, we are praying that God will be God. Next, we are to petition for God's moral order, God's justice: "Thy kingdom come, Thy will be done, on earth as it is in heaven." The coming kingdom will reestablish the absolute reign of God over his creation. Because Jesus has already inaugurated the kingdom, when we pray this prayer we are not only asking for his return, we are asking for the manifestation of God's kingdom now in our midst.

God's kingdom also includes prosperity. Thus, we are to pray, "Give us today our daily bread." While this may be a prayer for material blessing, it may also be better translated, "Give us tomorrow's bread [the bread or manna of the

Messiah, see John 6:32-35] today."⁹ This would mean that we are petitioning for the full salvation blessing of the Messiah to be ours now. Moreover, we are to receive God's mercy and then give it to each other, "And forgive us our debts, As we also have forgiven our debtors."

Finally, God's rule makes us secure. Thus, we are to ask, "Do not lead us into temptation [literally, do not let us fall victim to the eschatological trials or testing before the end, i.e., apostasy], But deliver us from evil," or better, "deliver us from the evil one." We ask God to be our Warrior-King by protecting us from the final tribulation and rescuing us from the devil. The ascription now appropriately stands, "For Thine is the kingdom, and the power and the glory forever. Amen." As Jesus ministers, Jesus teaches; and as Jesus teaches, Jesus prays. And as his disciples, so are we to pray. This prayer is our kingdom prayer.

The New Covenant

The description of Jesus' ministry would be incomplete without acknowledging that he is both the Warrior-King and the Suffering Servant. How do his power and his humiliation connect? The answer lies in Jesus' mission; he has come to defeat all of our enemies and to reclaim us for himself. Our great enemies, however, are sin, Satan, and judgment (death). Thus, for Jesus to be our Savior he must become our sacrifice. This is the reason that he goes to the cross.

In reestablishing God's kingdom, Jesus establishes a new covenant (Jer 31:31-34; Lk 22:20). Just as God called Abraham and made a covenant with him and just as he delivered Israel and made a covenant with her—so now Jesus calls his disciples and makes God's final covenant with them. While this covenant is like a "royal grant," unconditional, gracious, and binding, it also transcends all the former covenants and fulfills them. In the new covenant, God's promise to bless the nations in Abraham is fulfilled. In it the Mosaic demand for our absolute obedience is also fulfilled. And in it God's intention to reestablish his direct reign among his people and to honor his covenant with David, by placing his heir upon his throne forever, is fulfilled. This new covenant transcends all the others because it is internal rather than external, written upon the heart (Jer 31:33). Furthermore, rather than being for Israel alone (particular), it is for all the nations (universal).

It was this simple message of the cross that hooked me over thirty-five years ago. Gathered with several hundred other high school students, I heard Jim Rayburn, gifted evangelist to teens and the founder of Young Life, paint in dramatic strokes the final hours of Jesus' life. He described graphically how he was mocked, spit upon, and rejected by both Jews and Romans. He told us how he laid his naked body down upon rough boards and was nailed there quivering, still alive. He pictured him then hanging between heaven and earth.

Rayburn went on, "There were two groups of people at the cross. First, there was the crowd: the soldiers, the religious leaders who cried, 'Crucify him, Crucify him!' Second, there was a small group of women, and the Apostle John who went to the cross, not to mock, but to kneel and pray, and there was the dying thief who said, 'Lord, remember me when you come into your kingdom.'"

Rayburn concluded, "You are in one group or another. You are either saying, in effect, 'Jesus, stay on that cross and stay out of my life,' or 'Lord, remember me....' There is no fence to sit on because there is no fence." Brokenhearted, I knew that I had never come to the cross to pray, so, by definition, I was in the other group, the rejecting crowd. Gripped by Jesus' love, that night I came to the cross and as I did the kingdom came to me.

Granted that the kingdom is for us, how can we reveal its transforming power to the world? Can we declare the message of Jesus today without manifesting the ministry of Jesus? Are we left simply with his gospel and his ethics, or are we still to come against the powers of darkness in his name?

NINE

Imitators of Christ: The Ministry of the Church

TO WHAT EXTENT IS THE MINISTRY OF JESUS to be our ministry today? In what sense has the kingdom come for us? Few would dispute that we should do what Jesus did in building the church and evangelizing the world. The real battle rages over whether we should drive out demons, heal the sick, liberate the oppressed, and expect other signs and wonders such as Jesus' miracles over nature. Related to this is whether we, like Jesus and the apostles, can have a special anointing of the Spirit for such a ministry and whether all of the gifts of the Spirit, including tongues, prophecy, and healing, are available for us today as well.

That these questions are not academic is illustrated by the controversy which raged at Fuller Theological Seminary over John Wimber teaching a course in signs, wonders, and church growth. The book *Ministry and the Miraculous,* which resulted from the cancellation of his class, holds the traditional position that God grants signs and wonders to authenticate his Word. As David Hubbard, the President of Fuller, writes in the foreword, "The theological conclusion to be drawn from the Bible's own use of the miraculous seems clear; the primary motive for divine miracle is not compassion [in manifesting

God's kingdom] but revelation."[1] To substantiate this, the Fuller scholars argue that signs and wonders cluster around key redemptive events such as the Exodus and Jesus' ministry. Thus, they conclude that the concept of signs and wonders is narrowly employed in the Bible, and should not be used to describe the miraculous today.[2] Moreover, while the supernatural aspects of Jesus' ministry and the ministry of the apostles extend beyond the first century, they are a minor theme.

Out of this study, then, a vision for ministry at Fuller Seminary emerges: "The minister of the gospel should major in the power that enables ordinary people to bear the cross and accept the burdens of suffering for the sake of doing God's will in a world that hungers for forgiveness, reconciliation, justice, peace, the feeding of the hungry, and the relief of the oppressed."[3]

My intention here is to take issue with this prevalent view. I believe that we should not only comfort the afflicted but also heal the affliction as the practical manifestation of God's kingdom in our midst. Using the Fuller position as typical of the mainline church, I will offer an historical, theological, and practical response to its thesis. Let us look at each of these in turn.

Beyond Revelation

The basis upon which Jesus intended to extend both his message and his ministry beyond himself is found, first of all, in his calling a number of men to be his apostles. Scholars have shown that the Hebrew title from which our word "apostle" comes was given to a person commissioned to be the legal representative of another. Thus, the rabbis concluded that "the one sent by a man is as the man himself."[4] This required, of course, that the person who was sent submit his will to the one sending him, faithfully carrying out his orders.

Likewise, the New Testament definition of an apostle is "a man who is sent, and sent with full authority," lawfully charged to represent Jesus' person and cause.[5] The twelve were formed neither by a special spiritual endowment nor by their own decision, but solely on the initiative of Jesus.[6] Thus by calling the apostles, Jesus restores charismatic leadership to Israel in order to carry out both his message and his ministry. As Mark tells us, he called the twelve "that they might be with Him, and that He might send them out to preach, and to have authority to cast out the demons" (Mk 3:14-15). Likewise, Luke reports, "And He [Jesus] called the twelve together, and gave them power and authority over all the demons, and to heal diseases. And He sent them out to proclaim the kingdom of God and to perform healing" (Lk 9:1-2). Furthermore, Matthew describes Jesus' commission as he sent them out: "And as you go, preach, saying, 'The kingdom of heaven is at hand.' Heal the sick, raise the dead, cleanse the lepers, cast out demons; freely you received, freely give" (Mt 10:7-8). For them the authority, the message, and the ministry of Jesus all go together in one package.

Moreover, the task of representing Jesus by preaching and healing is not restricted to the apostles. Luke recounts that he also appointed seventy others and sent them ahead of him two by two as his heralds. In each city they are to "heal those in it who are sick, and say to them, 'The kingdom of God has come near to you'" (Lk 10:9). They later return to him joyfully announcing, "Lord, even the demons are subject to us in Your name." In their triumph Jesus responds, "I was watching Satan fall from heaven like lightning." Here we see that his battle with the kingdom of darkness is now joined through them. He then adds, "Behold, I have given you authority to tread upon serpents and scorpions, and over all the power of the enemy, and nothing shall injure you. Nevertheless do not rejoice in this, that the spirits are subject to you, but rejoice that your names are recorded in heaven" (Lk 10:17-20). We can conclude from these passages that Jesus' kingdom ministry, his word and his work, is first exhibited by him and then reproduced in his followers.

Let us look at the common arguments against the above assertions which are advanced by the Fuller scholars. If, as many in the church believe, signs and wonders are given to authenticate revelation rather than to establish ministry, the apostles' and disciples' ministry is not for us today. What reasons then are offered to document this thesis? The first argument for this position is that foremost among Jesus' works was his "forgiving of people's sins"[7] rather than casting out demons and healing the sick. It is important to note, however, that forgiveness is never included in the Gospel summaries of his ministry (Mt 4:23, etc.). Thus, this position makes a theological judgment rather than an historical observation by placing forgiveness at the top of the list.

Second, this position warns that Christians should not expect too much worldly benefit (such as healings) since Jesus calls us to suffer.[8] However, granted that we are called to suffer, we live in a kingdom come and coming where God's reign is actually breaking in upon us. To stress suffering at the expense of healing is to deny the pragmatic reality of the kingdom in our midst.

Third, this position argues that signs and wonders have a narrow function; they signal that the kingdom is drawing near in the "unique acts of God in Jesus."[9] Therefore, to call healings and other miracles today signs and wonders is to cheapen these acts. But as we have seen, the kingdom is come as well as coming, and we should expect signs and wonders to continue because they not only reveal the kingdom, they *realize* the kingdom. Furthermore, as Acts asserts, it is the risen Lord who continues his ministry of signs and wonders in his church. To fail to recognize this is to cheapen not them but him.

Fourth, this position asserts that Jesus' mandate to the apostles to preach the kingdom and heal the sick was a "specific mission" with "limited objectives."[10] We will have reason to challenge this conclusion below. Let it suffice us here to say that this commission was no more specific and limited than the ministry of Jesus itself. What he did personally and what he did with his disciples hang or fall together.

Fifth, this position claims that there is no healing mandate in the Great Commission. This can be challenged, however, from the form of the Commission in Matthew 28:18-20, as we shall see.

Rather than the thesis that Jesus reproduced his kingdom ministry in the apostles in order to authenticate revelation, we hold that Jesus reproduced his kingdom ministry in them in order that they might be the authoritative instruments of that kingdom for their world and generations yet to come. His design was not only that they bear his authority but also manifest his ministry. The execution of this design can be best understood in the context of the cross-cultural ideal of education in antiquity.

True Discipleship

In the ancient world true teaching and learning, what we would call "discipleship" today, took place as the teacher trained his pupils to be like himself. That is, they were to emulate him in all that he said and did. Unlike the modern philosophy of education, the ancient purpose of education was not merely to learn facts, evaluate them critically, and reproduce them on an exam; the purpose of education was to become like your teacher. Thus, his character and his behavior were as important as his thoughts. As the first century Stoic philosopher Seneca writes to Lucilius:

> Of course... the living voice and the intimacy of a common life will help you more than the written word. You must go to the scene of the action, first, because men put more faith in their eyes than in their ears, and second, because the way is long if one follows precepts, but short and helpful, if one

follows patterns. Cleanthes could not have been the express image of Zeno, if he had merely heard his lectures; he shared his life, saw into his hidden purposes and watched him to see whether he lived according to his own rules. . . . It was not the classroom of Epicurus, but living together under the same roof, that made great men of Metodorus, Hermarchus, and Polyaenus.[11]

This same ideal was also dominant in Israel. For the Jews, their rabbis not only were to teach the law, they were to live the law. In fact, they were "living Torah (law)."[12] For example, Rabbi Akiba, a contemporary of the apostle Paul, came from a peasant family and only began his studies in his adult years. Later he reports to his disciples that he even followed his Rabbi Joshua into the privy where he "learned from him three good habits." They respond in surprise, wondering if his Rabbi wasn't offended by this. Akiba replies, "I considered everything part of the Torah and I needed to learn."[13] Now we can understand why the Gospel writers include so much information about what Jesus both said and did. All was "Torah," or revelation, for them. As John's Gospel asserts, Jesus is the eternal Word of God who speaks the words of God: "For He whom God has sent speaks the words of God; for He gives the Spirit without measure" (Jn 3:34). Moreover, he also does the works of God: "Truly, truly, I say to you, the Son can do nothing of Himself, unless it is something He sees the Father doing; for whatever the Father does, these things the Son also does in like manner" (Jn 5:19). Here, indeed, is the ultimate expression of living Torah in word and deed, right from the heart of God himself.

It is no surprise, then, that Jesus molds his disciples to be like himself. As he says, "A disciple is not above his teacher, nor a slave above his master. It is enough for the disciple that he become as his teacher, and the slave as his master. If they have called the head of the house Beelzebul, how much more the members of his household!" (Mt 10:24-25). Again he says, "A pupil is not above his teacher; but everyone, after he has been fully trained, will be like his teacher" (Lk 6:40). Moreover, this ideal is clearly expressed in John's Gospel when Jesus says, "As Me (referring to Himself) . . . so you (referring to the disciples)." For example, after Jesus washes the disciples' feet he says, "You call Me Teacher and Lord; and you are right, for so I am. If I then, the Lord and the Teacher, washed your feet, you also ought to wash one another's feet. For I gave you an example that you also should do as I did to you" (Jn 13:13-15; see 13:34; 17:18, 23; 20:21). Thus, Jesus is no abstract ideal or myth for John. His disciples are to bear his message and do his ministry: "Truly, truly, I say to you, he who believes in Me, the works that I do shall he do also" (Jn 14:12).

Jesus intends to reproduce himself in his disciples. He teaches them in order that they may become extensions of himself. In this context we can understand sayings such as, "The one who listens to you listens to Me, and the one who rejects you rejects Me; and he who rejects Me rejects the One who sent Me" (Lk 10:16). Again, "He who receives you receives Me, and he who receives Me receives Him who sent Me" (Mt 10:40). Furthermore, as we serve Jesus' disciples we serve him. Therefore, on the Day of Judgment, when he separates the sheep from the goats, he will welcome the sheep, saying, "For I was hungry, and you gave Me something to eat; I was thirsty, and you gave Me drink; I was a stranger, and you invited Me in; naked, and you clothed Me; I was sick, and you visited Me; I was in prison and you came to Me" (Mt 25:35-36).[14] But how was it that in serving the disciples, Jesus himself was served? He replies, "Truly I say to you, to the extent that you did it to one of these brothers of Mine, even the least of them, you did it to Me" (Mt 25:40). Jesus' disciples represent Jesus himself.

Did Jesus' reproduction of his ministry in his apostles end with them? No. According to the New Testament, the exalted Lord continues to gift his church with charismatic leaders. As Paul tells the Ephesians, he gives apostles, prophets, evangelists and pastor-teachers, in order to equip the saints, that is, the whole body of believers for ministry (Eph 4:7-12). This is no seasonal ("dispensational") gifting, restricted to the Apostolic Age. The Book of Acts hints at this when it shows us that the next generation of leadership, men such as Stephen, Philip, and Paul, continue to minister with signs and wonders in the power of the Spirit (see Acts 6:5, 8; 8:6-8; 13:8-12, etc.).

Rather than looking for the gifts which Jesus is giving to the members of his church, we often simply recruit people for particular offices or programs, trying to plug them into the system and keep them there. Then we wonder why they don't thrive, why they burn out, why they become destructive or leave. For example, in the past I have often asked people to serve on church boards because of their accomplishments in the business world. They bring money and prestige to our work. This success, however, may not only not qualify them for leadership in the church, it may actually disqualify them once their business practices are known. Such people can be often manipulative and demanding behind the scenes, forcing the church into a management mold. They tend to measure ministry by their "bottom line" of black ink rather than by the service of people's needs. Once again, I have often looked for professional teachers to work in the Sunday School. Here it is easy to confuse their skills with the gifting of the Holy Spirit, when only this gifting will build up the church. What is the alternative to this approach? It is to become a biblical church, to allow Jesus to give us his gifts and for us to receive them gladly. We must pray them into existence. Once this is done our only other job is to test and affirm what he gives, while we let him run his church once again. We must learn to be true disciples. This is the goal of the church and the key to its ministry.

Nothing Less Will Do

Since the charismatic leaders given by the risen Lord are also to be disciplers, then they, in turn, will invest themselves in those who are raised up by the Spirit. Thus, they will continue the chain of teaching and training into the next generation. Of necessity this means that the ministry of the kingdom will not end with the Apostolic Age, since, starting with the apostles, each generation will pass on its ministry to the next. To invest the message without the ministry would be meaningless in light of the cultural context, as we have seen, and it would also be an act of disobedience. This is made clear in the "Great Commission" which concludes Matthew's Gospel. The risen Lord appears to the apostles and commands them: "Go . . . make disciples of all the nations, baptizing them in the name of the Father and the Son and the Holy Spirit, teaching them to observe all that I commanded you" (Mt 28:19-20). And what is it that Jesus commands? In sum, in the context of Matthew, it is to preach the gospel of the kingdom, cast out demons, and heal the sick. To be a disciple of Jesus is to bear his message and continue his ministry. Nothing less will do.

Likewise, Paul also uses this model of teaching in his churches. Trained as a Pharisee, he transmits the tradition of Jesus and lives that tradition so he can be an example to others as he ministers in power. He tells the Romans, "For I will not presume to speak of anything except what Christ has accomplished through me, resulting in the obedience of the Gentiles by word and deed, in the power of signs and wonders, in the power of the Spirit" (Rom 15:18-19). Moreover, Paul expected his converts to minister in the same way. As he exhorts the Corinthians, "Be imitators of me, just as I also am of Christ" (1 Cor 11:1). To restrict this imitation to teaching doctrine or ethics, is to miss the point of discipleship in the ancient world. As Paul manifested the ministry of Jesus, so he expects his church to manifest that same ministry. For example, he expects a continuing work of signs and wonders among the Galatians as he asks, rhetorically, "Does He then, who provides you with the Spirit and works miracles among you, do it by the works of the Law, or by hearing with faith?" (Gal 3:5). Later, when he corrects abuses in Corinth, he never suggests that the powerful manifestations of the Spirit there are not of God. Furthermore, he exhorts the Ephesians to be "filled with the Spirit" (Eph 5:18), and warns the Thessalonians not to quench the Spirit, by despising "prophetic utterances" (1 Thes 5:19-20). Finally, he calls upon Timothy, his leader for the next generation of believers, to "kindle afresh the gift of God which is in you through the laying on of my hands" and adds, "For God has not given us a spirit of timidity [a demonic spirit of fear], but of power and love and discipline [the Holy Spirit]" (2 Tm 1:6-7).

We must also remember that it is the exalted Lord who continues his ministry not only through gifted leaders such as Peter and Paul but also through the whole church which is his living body. 1 Corinthians 12 makes it clear that this ministry includes the works of his kingdom. Paul describes various gifts of the Spirit such as prophecy, words of wisdom and knowledge, gifts of healing (plural), discernment of spirits, and effecting miracles which will equip the church to continue the signs and wonders which Jesus performed. Moreover, Paul teaches that these gifts are situationally given by the Holy Spirit (1 Cor 12:11) for ministry in the moment (1 Cor 14:24-25, 30).[15] They are also to be actively sought (1 Cor 14:1), to appear especially in the gathered, worshiping congregation, to be used to edify the whole church (1 Cor 14:26), to be given without prejudice of sex or riches or ethnic background, and to be exercised in love (1 Cor 13). By giving the gifts of the Spirit, Jesus continues his ministry through his whole church. Because of this gifting, every Christian has the potential to prophesy or heal the sick. Here, indeed, the priesthood of all believers and the ministry of the laity are functionally expressed. Now the gathered congregation becomes an exciting place to be. Who knows what the sovereign Lord will do when we meet? Without surrendering stated leadership, and combining both form and freedom, the Holy Spirit may gift anyone for a specific task or ministry. As the Spirit is again welcomed in our churches, our gatherings will no longer be routine or dull.[16]

The New Testament itself bears witness to the continuation

of the message and ministry of Jesus far beyond the twelve apostles. His assaults upon Satan's kingdom and the healing of God's fallen creation extend into the next generation (see Hebrews 2:3-4). Moreover, his ministry did not stop there. In the second century, it was continued by believers who exercised Jesus' authority over the kingdom of Satan. As Justin Martyr writes, "This Word went out to all nations over which the demons rule, as David testifies, 'The gods of the nations are demons.' And so it happened that many, powerfully gripped by his Word abandoned the demons whom they served. Now through Jesus they have come to believe in the Almighty God."[17] And how are the demons expelled? He continues, "For every demon is exorcised, conquered, and subdued in the very name of this Son of God."[18] Justin then concludes, "After all, many of our people (the Christians namely) have healed a great number of possessed persons who did not receive healing from any other exorcist, sorcerer, or herb doctor. They did this throughout the whole world, and even in your own capital city, by driving out the demons in the name of Jesus Christ."[19]

This attack upon the demons and their idols provoked a counterattack, resulting in the persecution of the Christians. Here was a real power encounter. Thus, Justin writes, "the evil demons try to kill us because they hate us and because they find suitable judges to act as their tools and servants. It is just as if the authorities were possessed by them."[20] In the midst of this assault, however, God reveals his faithfulness. For example, Polycarp, the martyred Bishop of Smyrna, is given a vision of his pillow burning while he is praying. He then says to those with him, "I must be burned alive" and goes confidently to his death.[21] As the Smyrnans say of their martyrs, "They proved to all of us that in the hour of their torture they were free of the body, or rather that the Lord Himself stood by them and talked with them."[22]

A further witness to the continuing signs and wonders in the second century appears in a well-known passage in Irenaeus, who was probably a native of Smyrna (in Asia Minor) and later became the Bishop of Lyons (in modern France). Here he argues against the heretics who claim to have the very nature of Christ. His answer is that they cannot have the nature of Christ without doing the works of Christ:

> Wherefore, also, those who are in truth, His disciples, receiving grace from Him, do in His name perform [miracles], so as to promote the welfare of other men, according to the gift which each one has received from Him. For some do certainly and truly drive out devils, so that those who have thus been cleansed from evil spirits frequently both believe [in Christ], and join themselves to the Church. Others have foreknowledge of things to come; they see visions, and utter prophetic expressions. Others still, heal the sick by laying their hands upon them, and they are made whole. Yea, moreover, as I have said, the dead even have been raised up, and remained among us for many years. And what shall I more say? It is not possible to name the number of the gifts which the Church, [scattered] throughout the whole world, has received from God, in the name of Jesus Christ.... [But] directing her prayers to the Lord, who made all things ... and calling upon the name of our Lord Jesus Christ, she has been accustomed to work miracles for the advantage of mankind.[23]

Thus, the generations which followed the Apostolic Age experienced the risen Lord performing his signs and wonders in the midst of his people, engaging in spiritual warfare against the devil and all of his works.

Theological Stakes

What is at issue theologically by insisting that the church must bear the kingdom message and ministry of Jesus? First of all, our understanding of God himself is at stake, since the message of the kingdom presupposes that he is King. Moreover, his reign will come upon us as it is proclaimed in the power of the Spirit and we respond in faith (Gal 3:5). As this happens, we will begin to know God experientially as he is, in his heavenly glory, and be caught up before him in vital worship. The sense of his sovereignty, justice, and free grace will be restored to the church. At the same time, we will not shrink from also declaring his holy wrath, since he is also the Warrior-King who has come to defeat Satan's strongholds and judge the nations.

Furthermore, we will insist that God's kingdom has now been established in his Son overcoming all that transpired in the Fall. Rather than being satisfied with the Word of God alone, we will expect to see the work of God. Faith will not be left dangling and disembodied in an upper storey of idealism or mythological thinking. Since God has restored his rightful, direct reign among his people, we will receive the evidence of that reign. At the same time, we will also experience the tension of living in a kingdom both come and coming, which lies at the heart of the New Testament.

We will experience the presence of the kingdom in the free grace of Christ, the new birth, the empowering and the gifts of the Spirit, the authority of Jesus over the forces of darkness, the joy of a community of love, and certain hope for the future. At the same time, we will also experience the warfare of the flesh against the spirit, the seductions of the devil, the sufferings of physical limitations and debilitations, fightings without and fears within, and the "body of this death" (Rom 7:24) as we await the return of our Lord which will consummate his kingdom. For example, I know several people who have been healed of cancer directly and dramatically through prayer, including an elder of my former church whose tumor was dissolved the night before surgery. I also know several others, like my father-in-law and my brother-in-law who have died painful deaths because of this dread disease. It was in this context that I was asked to pray for the healing of a young girl suffering from advanced leukemia. A small team from our church spent the final days of her life with her. As we prayed she entered into a personal relationship with Jesus. In that time, her father also followed her into the faith, and the family was able to pray together at last. When the final hour came, as her parents held her in their arms and wept with both sorrow and joy, she vividly described Jesus coming to take her home. Our prayers for her healing were not answered as we would have liked, nevertheless, we saw God work in her situation in very real ways. In this age we must be prepared to live in the tension of the kingdom which is in our midst and yet not consummated. If we break it, we will end up either in a perfectionist theology, believing that the kingdom is now fully here, or in stoicism or cynicism, reflecting our doubt that the kingdom has ever come. History shows us that the church has often fallen prey to these errors, and we must stand militantly against them both.

Since this is a planet in revolt, we will especially expect to see God's reign through signs and wonders triumphing over the kingdom of the evil one, like the Christians of the first and second centuries did. Jesus has come to retrieve our birthright which was stolen by the devil. Although Satan has been defeated, the war continues. But it is clear that with the arrival of God's kingdom Satan's position in heaven and on earth has been decisively changed. Thus, as we have seen, when the disciples subject demons in his name, Jesus replies, "I was watching Satan fall from heaven like lightning" (Lk 10:18). Since the devil's activities are not limited to the Apostolic Age (he is no "dispensationalist"), we continue to need the powerful manifestation of God's authority in our age in order to overcome his works.

What we see in the ministry of Jesus, then, is the operative reign of God reclaiming the planet and reestablishing our reign in himself. Paul expresses this as he describes Christ as the perfect man, the second Adam, who inaugurates a whole new race (Rom 5:12-21). Thus, those who are *in* him will reign in life *through* him (Rom 5:17). As we stand before our pharaoh, he sends the plagues. As we march around our

Jericho, he brings down the walls. No wonder the demons cry out: "What do we have to do with You, Jesus of Nazareth? Have You come to destroy us? I know who You are—the Holy One of God!" (Mk 1:24, compare Mark 5:7).

With the New Testament we must conclude that Jesus has come to release Satan's stranglehold on this planet. As 1 John 3:8 expresses it, "The Son of God appeared for this purpose, that He might destroy the works of the devil." Both directly in power encounters, and indirectly as we battle against this world programmed by the enemy, we are engaged in this spiritual warfare. Thus, Paul writes, "For our struggle is not against flesh and blood, but against the rulers, against the powers, against the world forces of this darkness, against the spiritual forces of wickedness in the heavenly places" (Eph 6:12). In delivering people from demons, healing the sick, bringing justice to the oppressed, and bearing the gospel to the nations, we are rolling back the devil's kingdom and manifesting the kingdom of God. As a result, by his mercy we will experience authentic worship, receive his moral order, and be blessed by his prosperity and security as the expression of his reign restored over us.

One further point must be made here. The Messianic Age is the age of the Spirit. No wonder the New Testament is alive with his ministry. Thus, as we have seen, it is the Spirit who conceives Jesus in Mary's womb and descends upon him at his baptism. Again, it is the Spirit who sends him out on his messianic mission, empowering him to teach with authority and to heal the sick. The Spirit then falls upon the disciples at Pentecost, filling them again and again for spiritual battle. According to the Book of Acts and the Epistles, he leads the church in evangelizing the world and releases his gifts in her midst. Indeed, what Joel promised in the Old Testament and what Peter proclaimed on the day of Pentecost is true:

"And it will come about after this
That I will pour out My Spirit on all mankind;
And your sons and daughters will prophesy,

> Your old men will dream dreams,
> Your young men will see visions.
> And even on the male and female servants
> I will pour out My Spirit in those days." (Jl 2:28-29)

The Spirit may, in A.W. Tozer's words, be the neglected person of the Godhead, and it may well be today that we can only be called "Trinitarian" out of courtesy, but in the first century this was hardly so.[24] At the same time, wherever the church is being renewed, the powerful presence of the Spirit is being experienced once again.

There is no doubt, that we must have both the authority of Jesus and the power of the Holy Spirit in order to minister effectively against the devil and manifest the kingdom of God. To think otherwise is neither to know God nor our enemy. Do we bow before some "lesser god," one irrelevant to the real battle for this world?

A Practical Ministry

The Fuller study asserts that "the minister of the gospel should major in the power that enables ordinary people to bear the cross and accept the burdens of suffering for the sake of doing God's will."[25] While having sympathy with its intention, I find this view less and less acceptable biblically, theologically, and pastorally. How can we see the physical, emotional, and moral pain of people and adopt such a stoic attitude? What do we have to say to people trapped in compulsive sickness and sin? Is there any real healing for victims of child abuse, incest, alcoholism, and a variety of addictive behaviors? What do we have to offer to people who are judged terminally ill by the medical community? In my own ministry on the streets of Hollywood, I saw many come to Christ but then fall away because they found little power by simply reading their Bibles, attending church, fellowshiping with other Christians, and waiting for the Rapture—"to bear the cross and accept the burdens of suffering for the sake of doing God's will." What they needed was not more discipline. They needed Jesus' kingdom ministry. Some needed to be delivered from demons and all needed to be healed. I was not prepared for this. My agenda for ministry came from traditional evangelicalism, reflected in the Fuller study, rather than from Jesus.

If we adopt Jesus' agenda for ministry, we will pray down the anointing power of God, and with his Spirit upon us evangelize the poor, bring release to the captives, recovery of sight to the blind, liberate the oppressed, and announce to the world, this is "the favorable year of the Lord" (Lk 4:18-19). But how does this ministry work today? Here is where the change in my worldview impacts my own life and behavior.

In the opening chapter, I described my experience of the empowering of the Holy Spirit. In the last several years as I have laid hands upon people and prayed for them, I have seen that same Spirit come down upon them in power. Some have stood transfixed. Others have collapsed to the floor. Others have broken out in tongues or begun to prophesy. After I preached on the power of the Spirit one afternoon and the church stood to pray for him to come, my brother-in-law, Ron Rimmer, felt the Spirit fall upon him and course through him like a bolt of electricity. He stood with tears streaming down his cheeks. Someone nearby said, "Speak in tongues." He thought, "Speak in tongues! I can raise the dead!" His life has never been the same. There have also been occasions when I prayed and nothing happened. Sometimes I have found out later that indeed things did happen after some delay. However, we always minister within the sovereignty of God in a kingdom come and coming. People may be healed or they may not. God is the one who decides, but we are his servants to bring healing if God so desires.

Years ago, evangelizing the poor took me to the streets of Hollywood. Now in the '80s, this aspect of ministry has taken me to drug addicts, runaways, and "throwaways" on the streets of affluent La Jolla. Because of the abuse they have both received and given, they are often hardhearted and suspicious. Their underlying question is, "What do you want from me?" A tract will not do. Since the presence and power of Jesus must be seen in us by them, this ministry is time-intensive. What I can say is that in the moment of their brokenness, realizing that they have nothing, their hearts often open to him. I have seen prostitutes, cocaine addicts, heroin addicts, alcoholics, homosexuals, and all kinds of battered people come to Jesus right in La Jolla. Even with the power of the Spirit, however, such ministry is often heartbreaking. But apart from the power of the Spirit it is futile. Since the poor are upon Jesus' heart, when we let him, he puts them upon ours as well.

As we have seen from Luke 4, Jesus comes to bring "release to the captives." He comes to expell the demons. Believing this led me, along with Dr. Joe Ozawa, a psychologist, to pray with a friend of mine addicted to cocaine. As we ministered during the next two hours, several demons came out of him, some with violence. The result was that his ten-year, addictive compulsion to do drugs was broken in one night. From experiences such as this, I have come to believe that demons ride upon the drugs and that in many "incurable" cases, there is the need for deliverance.[26] The good news is that Jesus (and he alone) sets people free from these dark, supernatural powers.

Furthermore, Jesus comes to bring "recovery of sight to the blind." This promise represents his whole healing ministry which, as I noted above, I have begun to see in the church today. For example, I was visiting an older man a few months after we hosted a healing conference. As I was about to leave, Charles stopped me and said, "By the way, I haven't told you about my healing." He went on to relate that he had broken all the small bones in one wrist, which had then become inoperable and swollen to twice its normal size. At the conference, however, during a time for physical healing, people laid hands upon him and prayed and the chronic pain vanished. Then, the next day, when he awoke, the swelling was gone. Moreover, over a ten-day period every bone was healed.

The doctors at the Veterans Administration Hospital who were working with him were dumbfounded, as Charles had the joy of relating to them that Jesus had healed his wrist. When he told me this the tears streamed down his cheeks. Who says that signs and wonders merely prove revelation rather than actualize redemption? You can't tell Charles that! He won't believe you.

Finally, Jesus' agenda for ministry is to "set free the downtrodden." This means that he has come to liberate us from social, political, and economic bondage. As we attack these forms of oppression, represented by poverty, racism, and the arms race, we will also be coming against the evil principalities and powers which lie behind them. This is why social change becomes so intense, for it confronts the vested interests of both the natural and supernatural realms. A very personal example of this comes from the experience of two dear friends, Cindy and Rocky. My friend Rocky farms large tracts of land in Mexico with national partners. About three years ago his cash payroll of $30,000 vanished and the man delivering it was murdered. Flying south of the border to investigate, Rocky himself vanished. His wife Cindy called in desperation on a Saturday night, fearing that he was dead. We learned later that the state police had stolen the money and killed its courier. They then held Rocky handcuffed and blindfolded in a house awaiting certain death. Here the principalities and powers, working through the order of the state and human greed, were in operation. We prayed off and on through the night for Rocky. The next morning Cindy came to church, unnoticed by me, and wept softly in the back through the service. As she was leaving, a young man named Mike came up to her, having received a word from the Lord while he sat behind her, and said apologetically, "I've never done anything like this before, and I don't understand it, but does 'He'll be back' mean anything to you?" With this Cindy completely broke down, and within two days, Rocky was returned to the States. As a footnote to the story, he had been praying that Sunday morning in Mexico, "Lord, let my wife know that I am alive." Through his Spirit, Jesus frees the downtrodden. Evangelism, deliverance, healing, and liberation: this is his agenda for ministry. It was also the agenda of the early church far into the second century. Is it ours?

As we consider our answer, objections quickly arise. What about those who pray for the power of the Spirit and nothing happens (remember that the apostles prayed for ten straight days before Pentecost)? What about those who are not delivered or healed? What about those who die under oppression, even as the martyrs, rather than walk out alive? Part of our answer to these questions certainly rests in the sovereignty of God. While Peter escaped prison unharmed through angelic intervention, Stephen died under a hail of stones. In both cases, however, the Lord was glorified through them. Part of our answer also lies in our own sin which can be a barrier to healing. God may not heal us because in his "passive wrath" he wants to bring us to repentance. We must also acknowledge the limited successes of the devil who is still our active antagonist against God's kingdom triumphing in us. Furthermore, we are often a house divided against ourselves because of the brainwashing of the Enlightenment and the weakness of a worldly church. To pray in simple faith, we must recover the "Christian mind." We must also remember that not even Jesus could do his mighty works in Nazareth because of their unbelief (Mk 6:1-6). Could this not also be said of London, Moscow, or New York as well? Finally, we must remember that we live in the kingdom come and coming. Our experiences of the power and authority of that kingdom will assure us that God is at work in our world. However, our failure to experience the fullness of that kingdom will keep our eyes fixed upon the future. We will be a church which has become an instrument of the kingdom and, at the same time, one that awaits that kingdom yet to come where Jesus will consummate his reign and God will be all in all (1 Cor 15:24-28).

TEN

Come, Lord Jesus

AS HISTORY RUSHES TOWARD ITS CLIMAX with superpower face-offs, crushing international debt, and pollution and population verging out of control, we must remember that God is King. In his Son Jesus, we have the presence of his kingdom intersecting our lives and the promise of its future consummation. This may be troubling for some of us because of our anti-supernatural bias, but our trouble doesn't make it any less true. The major themes of prophetic thought within which Jesus operated are not some apocalyptic aberration but dominate the whole Bible. These include God enthroned in heaven surrounded by his holy angels, his sovereign reign over the cosmos, his mighty acts in signs and wonders, the Day of Judgment, and his renewed kingdom. Our Lord's whole life was determined by this sense of God's rule which will be consummated with a great finale, when the "End of the end" breaks in upon us. He died to prepare us for that finale—the Day of Judgment. Moreover, his victory over the grave is no isolated event. It is the "first fruits" of the general resurrection of the dead. As we lower our loved ones into the earth, the fact that Jesus lives is the one assurance which we have that they too will be raised when he returns. But what is our Lord's specific vision of the future? We can answer this simply: He looks forward to the full establishment of God's kingdom reign and rule on this planet and over the whole cosmos.

The Kingdom Consummated

There will be a day when Jesus returns as the glorified Son of Man (compare Daniel 7:13-14). In his visible, triumphant appearing, he will raise the believing dead and transform the living (1 Thes 4:13ff). He will defeat Satan and his political world ruler Antichrist, judge the nations, and manifest his complete reign over the kingdom of darkness. As a result, the whole cosmos will ring with worship. His coming again will take place when the Great Commission is fulfilled. As Jesus promises, "And this gospel of the kingdom shall be preached in the whole world for a witness to all the nations, and then the end shall come" (Mt 24:14). While we are not to *predict* when He will return, we are to *prepare* for his return (see Acts 1:7-8). Now, at last, all will see that he is King.

God's historical judgment is one of the signs of the end (Mt 24:1-2). This judgment has already fallen upon Jerusalem when it was destroyed by the Roman general Titus in A.D. 70. As Jesus warns the Pharisees, "Therefore I say to you, the kingdom of God will be taken away from you, and be given to a nation producing the fruit of it" (Mt 21:43). This awesome truth, however, breaks his heart as he weeps over the holy city: "O Jerusalem, Jerusalem. . . . How often I wanted to gather your children together, the way a hen gathers her chicks under her wings, and you were unwilling. Behold, your house is being left to you desolate!" (Mt 23:37-38).

The destruction of Jerusalem meant the destruction of the temple, the slaughter of the priesthood, and the abolition of the sacrificial system. All of this is a consequence of Israel rejecting her Messiah. Because access to God has been fulfilled by Jesus' death on the cross, the old rituals are useless and vanish from history. While God now undertakes the conversion of the Gentiles, he still has a plan for his people Israel. Thus, as Paul says, when "the fullness of the Gentiles" has come in, he will keep his unconditional promise to the Jews, and all Israel will be saved (see Romans 11). Jew and Gentile, then, will be united in the kingdom of God.

In the meantime, Satan continues his attacks. As Jesus warns, false Messiahs and false prophets will come, even with signs and wonders, and mislead many (Mt 24:5, 11, 24). Lawlessness will also increase and (as a result) love will grow cold (Mt 24:12). Nevertheless, God still runs his world. Thus, he sends his judgments: wars and rumors of wars, famines and earthquakes (Mt 24:6-7). These four horsemen of the Apocalypse (Rv 6:1-8), will be followed by "a great tribulation, such as has not occurred since the beginning of the world until now, nor ever shall" (Mt 24:21). The final birth pangs which herald the end, however, are shortened for the sake of the elect (Mt 24:8, 22). Great judgments will rain down upon the earth, even as the plagues rained down upon Pharaoh, and like him, the rest of mankind will not repent (Rv 9:20-21).

The Book of Revelation shows that these catastrophies will escalate before the final cosmic collapse. Then all people great and small will say to the mountains and the rocks, "Fall on us and hide us from the presence of Him who sits on the throne [God], and from the wrath of the Lamb [Jesus]; for the great day of their wrath has come; and who is able to stand?" (Rv 6:16-17; compare Isaiah 2:19-21).

At this point Jesus will appear, riding a white horse:

> And He who sat upon it is called Faithful and True; and in righteousness He judges and wages war. And His eyes are a flame of fire, and upon His head are many diadems; ... And He is clothed with a robe dipped in blood; and His name is called The Word of God [see John 1:1]. And the armies which are in heaven [the angels], clothed in fine linen, white and clean, were following Him on white horses. And from His mouth comes a sharp sword, so that with it He may smite the nations; and He will rule them with a rod of iron; and He treads the wine press of the fierce wrath of God, the Almighty [see Isaiah 63:1-6]. And on His robe and on His thigh He has a name written, "KING OF KINGS, AND LORD OF LORDS." (Rv 19:11-16, see 2 Thessalonians 1:6-10)

Final Judgment

After his triumphal appearance, Jesus will act as Judge and hold his final court. Thus, he teaches his disciples that the kingdom of heaven is like a man who sowed good seed in his field while an enemy sowed tares. The wheat and the tares grew up together until the harvest. He continues, "... as for the good seed, these are the sons of the kingdom; and the tares are the sons of the evil one ... and the harvest is the end of the age; and the reapers are angels" (Mt 13:38-39). Jesus concludes: "The Son of Man will send forth His angels, and they will gather out of His kingdom all stumbling blocks, and those who commit lawlessness, and will cast them into the furnace of fire; in that place there shall be weeping and gnashing of teeth. Then the righteous will shine forth as the sun in the kingdom of their Father ..." (Mt 13:41-43).

This final judgment is described in Matthew 25. There Jesus says,

> "But when the Son of Man comes in His glory, and all the angels with Him, then He will sit on His glorious throne. And all the nations will be gathered before Him; and He will separate them from one another, as the shepherd separates the sheep from the goats." (Mt 25:31-32)

The sheep, who are the righteous, are welcomed: "Then the King will say to those on his right, 'Come, you who are blessed of My Father, inherit the kingdom prepared for you from the foundation of the world'" (Mt 25:34). And why are they welcomed? Because, as they served Jesus' disciples, they served him, displaying their true righteousness and proving that they belonged to him. The goats, however, are rejected because they rejected Jesus' disciples. Thus, he concludes, "And these will go away into eternal punishment, but the righteous into eternal life" (Mt 25:46). This eternal judgment, however, is not just for unrighteous people, it is also for God's cosmic enemies who have wreaked such havoc upon the earth, namely, the devil and his angels (Mt 25:41). Thus, John tells us, "And the devil ... was thrown into the lake of fire and brimstone, where the beast [Antichrist, Rv 13:1ff], and the false prophet [Rv 13:11ff] are also; and they will be tormented day and night forever and ever" (Rv 20:10). After this final separation, Jesus promises that the righteous will shine like the sun in the kingdom of their Father (Mt 13:43). All of this reveals that Jesus is King. He defeats his enemies, executes the final judgment, and welcomes the righteous into his glory.

Visions of Eternity

What then is the final, biblical vision of the future? In light of our previous study, we are not surprised to find that God's kingdom contains ecstatic worship, perfect order, complete prosperity, and eternal security.

First, in the Book of Revelation, the final events of the end are laced with heavenly worship. Windows are opened, showing us the saints responding to God's reign by casting their crowns before him. Before "the throne of God and of the Lamb ... His bond-servants shall serve Him" (Rv 22:3). Their service is worship, the offering of praise to him as Creator and Redeemer:

> After these things I [John] looked, and behold, a great multitude, which no one could count, from every nation and all tribes and peoples and tongues, standing before the throne and before the Lamb, clothed in white robes, and palm branches were in their hands; and they cry out with a loud voice, saying, "Salvation to our God who sits on the throne, and to the Lamb." And all the angels were standing around the throne and around the elders and the four living creatures; and they fell on their faces before the throne and worshiped God, saying, "Amen, blessing and glory and wisdom and thanksgiving and honor and power and might, be to our God forever and ever. Amen." (Rv 7:9-12)

All lesser gods are dust. God alone is King. In these final visions he is no longer hidden in awesome majesty. Unlike Moses, we shall see his face and live (Rv 22:4). This is the fulfillment of our salvation and our souls. In *The City of God*, Augustine expresses this reality,

> Our heart when it rises to Him is His altar; the priest who intercedes for us is His Only-begotten; . . . to Him we offer the sweetest incense when we come before Him burning with holy and pious love; to Him we devote and surrender ourselves and His gifts in us; . . . to Him we offer on the altar of our heart the sacrifice of humility and praise. . . . For He is the fountain of our happiness, He is the end of all our desires. . . . [By] being re-attached to Him, we tend towards Him by love, that we may rest in Him, and find our blessedness. . . . For our good . . . is nothing else than to be united to God.[1]

Second, God establishes perfect order by creating a new heaven and a new earth in which righteousness dwells (2 Pt 3:13). There his will will be finally and fully done. To share in the new earth we shall receive our resurrection bodies which will be like the glorious body of Jesus himself (Rom 6:5; 8:11). Then, the full image of God given in creation will be restored as we are conformed to Christ, the second Adam (2 Cor 3:18; 1 Cor 15:45-49). Moreover, complete dominion over the planet will again be ours when we reign with Christ over His realm (Rom 8:17; Eph 2:6-7; compare Matthew 20:20-23). This is pure theocracy.

Third, in God's kingdom there is complete prosperity. God as King will pour his bounty upon us. The new earth will be a new Eden, the garden of God, with a "river of the water of life" and "the tree of life, bearing twelve kinds of fruit, yielding its fruit every month; and the leaves of the tree were for the healing of the nations" (Rv 22:1-2). Now the cleansed and regenerated earth will bloom.

As sons and daughters of the King we will eat and drink anew with Jesus in the kingdom of God (Mt 26:29). As the Book of Revelation promises, we will join in the marriage supper of the Lamb (Rv 19:7-9) when Christ, the bridegroom, is reunited to the church, his bride, "having no spot or wrinkle or any such thing" (Eph 5:27). Here we will experience the full blessing of God.

Fourth, Jesus guarantees our security in the kingdom for eternity. All our enemies, natural and supernatural, will be vanquished. As we have seen, Satan and his demonic agents are cast into the lake of fire. Sin and death will also be destroyed (Rv 20:14). Thus, John writes, "But for the cowardly and unbelieving and abominable and murderers and immoral persons and sorcerers and idolaters and all liars, their part will be in the lake that burns with fire and brimstone, which is the second death" (Rv 21:8). Now the redeemed will shine. As the final visions of the Revelation show: "He shall wipe away every tear from their eyes; and there shall no longer be any death; there shall no longer be any mourning, or crying, or pain; the first things have passed away." John continues, "And He who sits on the throne said, 'Behold, I am making all things new'" (Rv 21:4-5). No wonder the gates of the New Jerusalem are always open. There is no need to shut them out of fear again (Rv 21:27). The prayer that Jesus taught us to pray will be fully answered, "Thy kingdom come, Thy will be done, on earth as it is in heaven."

The Streaks of Dawn

Karl Barth notes that morality demands at least a pinch of the apocalyptic. In other words, our behavior now will be determined, at least in part, by our grasp of the judgment to come. Since one day we will account for our lives before God, how then are we to live?

Jesus tells us that we are to be on the alert. We are to be like the wise virgins who have an ample supply of oil for their lamps and are ready for the bridegroom's midnight return (Mt 25:6). With a "Christian mind" illumined by the totality of biblical revelation, we are to know the signs of the times (Mt 24:3-4) and watch and pray lest we enter into temptation (Mt 26:41). Having surrendered our autonomy, we are to be busy about our Lord's business, investing the talents which he has given us in order to earn him a return (Mt 25:14-30). And what is his business? It is the evangelization of the world. Jesus says, "... this gospel of the kingdom shall be preached in the whole world for a witness to all the nations, and then the end shall come" (Mt 24:14). The completion of the Great Commission is the only thing which delays his return.

One of the most remarkable facts today is the growing resolve across the church to reach the world by year A.D. 2000. The great watchword of the Student Volunteer Movement at the turn of the century, "the evangelization of the world in this generation," has been refocused on the end of this century. David Hesselgrave, Professor of Missions at Trinity Evangelical Divinity School, notes that this is more than rhetoric. The reason for this is that we now have a much better idea of what an evangelized world would look like since we know that there are 17,000 people groups with distinct cultures which have yet to hear the gospel and have any active church in their midst. Reaching them is our priority. We also know better what we mean by "evangelized." There is a growing consensus that people are reached when they have understood the gospel and when an evangelizing church is geographically and culturally accessible to them. But can this be done by the year 2000? The fact is that we have made great progress during the twentieth century. David Barett, editor of the *World Christian Encyclopedia,* calculates that at the year 1900 51.3 percent of the world had been evangelized. However, by 1986 72.7 percent had been reached with a hearing of the gospel. Another remarkable reality of our times is that churches in the Third World have raised up at least 20,000 non-Western missionaries and that this force will grow to 100,000 by the end of this century.

Ralph Winter, the founder of the U.S. Center for World Mission, also reports that the majority of the 17,000 unreached people groups have already been targeted for penetration by the gospel. Hesselgrave concludes, "World evangelization by the year 2000 is a realistic goal.... Perhaps to a degree that has never before been true in history, the church possesses the potential to accomplish [this goal] ... within a very limited period of time."[2] This is especially true, I may add, as God is pouring out his Spirit in power upon us and manifesting his kingdom presence by signs and wonders in our midst. We are to occupy ourselves, then, with the Great Commission and marshall our efforts to fulfill it until the Lord comes. This, however, will evoke the enemy's counterattack.

Because we are called to the trenches, we are to be the church suffering and militant in this world. We are to stay on the alert because we are at war (1 Thes 5:6). In this battle we must remember that deception is Satan's middle name. Most often he cunningly disguises himself as an angel of light (2 Cor 11:14). He is also a prowling lion hungry to devour us (1 Pt 5:8). However, we are not ignorant of his designs ("schemes," 2 Cor 2:11). Our posture in this world is not to be defensive. We are an offensive army, besieging the very gates of Hell (Mt 16:18), taking its captives for the kingdom of God, confident that nothing can separate us from the love of God which is in Christ Jesus our Lord (Rom 8:39). The Christian mission is the most remarkable historical movement of all time, and, since the gospel must be preached to all nations before the end comes, it is vitally on the march today.

At the very moment of our suffering in this world, we are also to know the touch of glory because we live in a kingdom both come and coming. Thus, God's Spirit is upon us. We have been sealed, anointed, and filled by him (Eph 1:13; 2 Cor 1:21-22; Acts 2:4). Knowing a joy unspeakable, we rejoice in our tribulations, for in them we share in the very sufferings of Christ himself. At the same time, we have entered into a new community of love and righteousness under the reign of God.

Here is the environment in which faith grows as we experience Jesus in our midst. Moreover, as we have seen, with his agenda for ministry we are to evangelize the poor, cast out demons, heal the sick, and set free the downtrodden. The church like this becomes the instrument of the kingdom and finds and fulfills her destiny. Jesus' triumph is ours and in these victories, however partial, we see the streaks of dawn breaking across the darkened sky. Indeed, as Paul tells the Romans, we know that the night is far spent and the day is at hand (Rom 13:12).

What, then, will be our own response to this critical moment before us for world evangelism? Never has the church lived in a time of such peril and such promise. For myself it is time to repent of my faint heart, my selfish, isolated "democratic personality," my relativism, my accommodation to our culture, and my latent anti-supernaturalism. It is time to embrace fully the "Christian mind" and to let the kingdom come. I want to join the great eighteenth century Anglican evangelist, George Whitefield, who preached the gospel to over half the English speaking world of his day, as he prayed: "God, give me a deep humility, a well-guided zeal, a burning love and a single eye, and, then let men or devils do their worst."[3]

As God answers, we will look up, bloody but unbowed, for our redemption draws near.

"Thy kingdom come. Thy will be done on earth . . ." Maranatha, come, Lord Jesus!

Chapter Notes

Chapter One

1. Francis Schaeffer, *Escape from Reason*, (Downers Grove, Illinois: Inter Varsity Press, 1968), p. 46.
2. *The Chief Works of Benedict De Spinoza*, tr. by R.H.M. Elwes, (New York: Dover Publications, 1951) Vol I, p. 83.
3. Edward Gibbon, *The Decline and Fall of the Roman Empire*, (New York: The Modern Library, n.d.), Vol. I, p. 407.
4. Ibid, p. 409.
5. Timothy Leary quote is taken from memory of an interview given years ago.
6. Carl Becker, *The Heavenly City of the Eighteenth-Century Philosophers*, (New Haven, Connecticut: Yale Univ. Press, 1932), p. 15.
7. Walter Wink, *The Bible in Human Transformation*, (Philadelphia: Fortress Press, 1973), p. 7.
8. Jonathan Edwards citation from D. Martin Lloyd-Jones, *Joy Unspeakable*, (Eastbourne, England: Kingsway Pub., 1984), p. 79.
9. Dwight Moody citation from D. Martin Lloyd-Jones, p. 80.
10. Michael Cassidy, *Bursting the Wineskins*, (London, England: Hodder & Stoughton, 1983), p. 122.
11. Jeremy Rifkin with Ted Howard, *The Emerging Order*, (New York: Putnam, 1979), p. x.

Chapter Two

1. See Fiske's article, "At 350, the U.S. University is Vast but Unfocused," in *The New York Times*, Sept. 7, 1986, p. 38.
2. Allan Bloom, *The Closing of the American Mind*, (New York: Simon and Schuster, 1987), p. 85.
3. Thus, feminists conclude, biology is not destiny. All that is left is a unisexual ideal transcending all gender distinctions.
4. Ibid,, p. 114.
5. John Wesley citation from D. Martyn Lloyd-Jones, p. 62.

Chapter Three

1. Harry Blamires, *The Christian Mind*, (Ann Arbor, Michigan: Servant Books, 1978), p. 4.
2. Allan Bloom, p. 58.
3. Hanry Bamford Parks, *Gods and Men: The Origins of Western Culture*, (New York: Knopf, 1959), p. 52.
4. Quotations which follow are taken from James Pritchard, *Ancient Near Eastern Texts*, 2nd edition, (Princeton, New Jersey: Princeton Univ. Press, 1955), pp. 163ff.
5. Ibid., pp. 163ff.
6. Ibid., pp. 163ff.
7. Ibid., pp. 163ff.
8. Ibid., pp. 163ff.
9. Starting with 1 Samuel, this title occurs throughout the period of the monarchy and beyond. It is used fifteen times in the psalter; once in Hosea, Micah, and Habakkuk; twice in Nahum; nine times in Amos; sixty-three times in Isaiah; eighty-three times in Jeremiah; fourteen times in Haggai; fifty-three times in Zechariah; and twenty-four times in Malachi. As A.A. Anderson notes, the main problem in interpreting the title lies in the meaning of "hosts." At times it clearly refers to the armies of Israel (Ex 7:4). At other times it includes the heavenly bodies or the armies of angels and other spiritual beings. Anderson concludes, "Perhaps the most likely explanation is the rendering 'Yahweh (whose are) the hosts (i.e. all the powers on earth and in heaven).'" A.A. Anderson, *The New Century Bible Commentary, Psalms (1-72)*, (Grand Rapids: Eerdmans, 1972), p. 206.
10. Antonia Fraser, ed., *The Lives of the Kings and Queens of England*, (New York: Knopf, 1975), p. 11.
11. Compare Proverbs 3:19, "The LORD by wisdom founded the earth" and John 1:1-3, "In the beginning was the Word.... All things came into being by Him."
12. Charles Kraft, "Shifting Worldviews, Shifting Attitudes," in Wimber and Springer, *Riding the Third Wave*, (Basingstoke, Hants: Marshall Pickering, 1987), pp. 123-124.
13. Ibid., pp. 133-134.

Chapter Four

1. M. Scott Peck, *People of the Lie, The Hope for Healing Human Evil*, (New York: Simon and Schuster, 1983), p. 10.
2. Ibid., p. 12.
3. Wade Davis, *The Serpent and the Rainbow*, (New York: Simon and Schuster, 1985), p. 51.
4. Don Williams, *Bob Dylan, The Man, The Music, The Message*, (Old Tappan, New Jersey: Revell, 1985), p. 87.
5. That is, in a rational sense. The Bible offers a descriptive and realistic view of evil and its conquest.

6. As Shirley MacLaine writes, "One of my great pleasures was having sessions with accredited 'mediums' who channeled the soul energy of beings from the spiritual plane who acted as guides and teachers.... A nice young man named Kevin Ryerson had found, some years ago, that he had the talent to attune his body frequencies to spiritual beings who themselves were no longer in the body. These beings used the electromagnetic frequencies of Kevin's body as a channel through which they could communicate with us on the earth plane from the spiritual plane where they resided. Kevin would go into a trance state while the spiritual beings used him as a medium through which to communicate." *Dancing in the Light,* (New York: Bantam Books, 1985), pp. 74-75.
7. Michael Green, *I Believe in Satan's Downfall,* (Grand Rapids: Eerdmans, 1981), p. 79.
8. Wimber and Springer, p. 98.
9. John White, *When the Spirit Comes with Power,* (Downers Grove, Illinois: InterVarsity Press, 1988), pp. 203-205.

Chapter Five

1. G. Johannes Botterweck and Helmer Ringgren, *Theological Dictionary of the Old Testament,* Vol. II, (Grand Rapids: Eerdmans, 1975), p. 271.
2. Since God is supreme He cannot swear by anything greater than Himself. As we have seen above, there is no appeal beyond Him.
3. Dietrich Bonhoeffer, *The Cost of Discipleship,* (New York: MacMillan, 1963), p. 4.
4. Carol Wimber, "A Hunger For God," in Wimber and Springer, pp. 36-37.
5. Tom Stipe, "Recovering the Ministry I Left Behind," in Wimber and Springer, p. 209.

Chapter Six

1. Up to a point, Satan can duplicate the works of God. The New Testament warns of false prophets who do mighty works in order to deceive even the elect (see 2 Thessalonians 2:9-10).
2. The common elements between the Mosaic covenant and the Hittite treaties include a title, followed by an historical introduction designed to motivate loyalty by recounting what the great King did for his vassal. Next, the stipulations of the treaty are listed and the gods are called to witness its execution. Blessings for obedience and curses for disobedience are then pronounced. The treaty is now publicly read before the people, recorded on tablets and deposited in an appropriate place. Weinfeld comments, "Indeed, the Sinai covenant described in Exodus 19-24 has a similar structure.... Thus, the divine address opens with an historical introduction stressing the grace of God with the people and their election (19:4-6); then follows the law (20:1-23:19); thereafter comes a series of promises and threats (23:20-33); and finally the

ratification of the covenant by means of a cultic ceremony [which includes the sprinkling of blood and a sacred meal] and the recital of the covenant document (24:3-11)." Botterweck and Ringgren, p. 266.
3. Carol Wimber, in Wimber and Springer, pp. 45-46.

Chapter Seven

1. "... a man in whom is the Spirit" (Nm 27:18).
2. Gideon experiences the "Spirit of the LORD" coming upon him as he prepares for battle (Jgs 6:34). This is also true for Jephthah (Jgs 11:29). Moreover, Samson tears a young lion apart when "the Spirit of the LORD came upon him mightily" (Jgs 14:6). Later, with the Spirit upon him, he kills thirty men at Ashkelon and another thousand at Lehi with the jawbone of a donkey (Jgs 14:19; 15:4-5).
3. That this is understood is clear from Gideon's response when Israel wants to make him king after Midian's defeat: "I will not rule over you, nor shall my son rule over you; the LORD shall rule over you" (Jdg 8:23).
4. Here we see that signs and wonders are the manifestation of the kingdom of God, i.e., God's reign in Israel. In this sense they do not accompany revelation or prove revelation, but they implement God's reign, as the instruments of his kingdom. No wonder they are restored in the ministry of Jesus!
5. In the period of the monarchy God's signs and wonders are often seen in acts of judgment. Modern dispensationalists fail to see this because they fail to understand the wrath of God.

Chapter Eight

1. Rudolf Bultmann, *Theology of the New Testament*, (New York: Scribners, 1951), Vol I, p. 4.
2. Albert Schweitzer, *The Quest of the Historical Jesus*, (New York: MacMillan, 1957), pp. 398-403.
3. See C.H. Dodd, *The Parables of the Kingdom*, (London: Nisbet, 1936). I am indebted to W.D. Davies for this insight.
4. See Oscar Cullmann, *Christ and Time*, (New York: Gordon Press, 1977). I am indebted to Cullmann for this analogy.
5. Jeremias notes, "Now wherever the Spirit of God is revealed in the biblical sphere, this happens in a twofold way, *en ergo kai logo* [in deed and word] (Lk 24:19; cf. Mk 1:27; 1 Thes 1:5, etc.). The two belong indissolubly together. The word is never without its accompanying deed and the deed is never without the word that proclaims it. So too with Jesus: the concluding revelation is manifested in two ways (see Matthew 11:5f): in acts of power and in words of authority," *New Testament Theology*, (New York: Scribners, 1971), p. 85.
6. Jesus calling his disciples is the opposite of the rabbis who waited for their disciples to join them. This makes him a "charismatic leader" rather than a mere teacher, see Martin Hengel, *The Charismatic Leader and His*

Followers, (New York: Crossroad, 1981).
7. Dietrich Bonhoeffer in *The Cost of Discipleship* notes that while Jews have a direct relationship to the law, Christians have an indirect relationship, mediated by Jesus.
8. Jeremias, p. 94.
9. See the comments on *epiousios* in Arndt and Gingrich, *A Greek-English Lexicon of the New Testament* (Chicago: Univ. of Chicago Press, 1957), in 4. d. "The petition is referred to the coming kingdom and its feast," p. 297. Jeremias notes, "This eschatological understanding of the petition for bread was the dominant one in the first centuries, both in East and in West," p. 200.

Chapter Nine

1. Lewis Smedes, ed., *Ministry and the Miraculous,* (Pasadena, CA: Fuller Theological Seminary, 1987), p. 13.
2. Ibid., p. 28.
3. Ibid., pp. 28-29.
4. Rengstorf, apostolos, in *Theological Dictionary of the New Testament*, Vol. I, (Grand Rapids: Eerdmans, 1964), p. 415.
5. Ibid., p. 421.
6. Ibid., p. 424.
7. Smedes, p. 25.
8. Ibid., p. 26.
9. Ibid., p. 28.
10. Ibid., p. 29.
11. Seneca, *Ad Lucilium Epistulae Morales,* Vi. 5-7.
12. B. Gerhardsson, *Memory and Manuscript,* (Uppsala: Almqvist and Wiksells, 1961), pp. 182ff.
13. Louis Finkelstein, *Akiba,* (New York: Covici, Friede, 1936), p. 181.
14. Quite certainly here Jesus is thinking of service to his itinerant missionaries which included providing food, clothing, and hospitality. When they were persecuted, they were to also be visited in prison.
15. I am dependent upon John Wimber for this insight.
16. D. Martyn Lloyd-Jones wisely comments, "People come to the New Testament and, instead of taking its teaching as it is, they interpret it in the light of their experience, and so they reduce it.... And I believe that this is very largely responsible for the condition of the Christian church at this present time. People are so afraid of enthusiasm, and some are so afraid of fanaticism, that in order to avoid those they go right over to the other side without facing what is offered in the New Testament. They take what they have and what they are as the norm.

"Let me just put it in a nutshell in this way. Compare, for instance, what you read about the life of the church at Corinth with typical church life today. 'Ah but,' you say, 'they were guilty of excesses in Corinth.' I quite agree. But how many churches do you know at the present time to which it is necessary to write such a letter as the First Epistle of Paul to

the Corinthians? Do not put your emphasis entirely on the excesses. Paul corrects the excesses but see what he allows, what he expects," ("Dialogue with Trypho," 83.4.), pp. 18-19.
17. Eberhard Arnold, *The Early Christians*, (Grand Rapids: Baker, 1979), p. 95.
18. *"Dialogue with Trypho,"* 85.1-2, in Ibid., p. 96.
19. *"Second Apology,"* 6, in Ibid., p. 138.
20. *"Second Apology,"* 1, 2, in Ibid., p. 84.
21. *"The Martyrdom of the Holy Polycarp"* in Ibid., p. 70.
22. Ibid., p. 66.
23. *Irenaeus Against Heresies*, XXXII.4, in *The Ante-Nicene Fathers*, (Grand Rapids: Eerdmans, 1981), Vol. I, p. 409.
24. Tozer writes, "... the doctrine of the Holy Spirit as held by evangelical Christians today has almost no practical value at all. In most Christian churches the Spirit is quite entirely overlooked. Whether he is present or absent makes no real difference to anyone." *A Treasury of A.W. Tozer*, (Harrisburg, Pennsylvania: Christian Pub., Inc., 1980), p. 40.
25. Smedes, pp. 28-29.
26. Eighty percent of the cocaine in the U.S.A. comes from Columbia which, as a missionary reported to me, has been a center of strong demonic activity for over a thousand years.

Chapter Ten

1. Saint Augustine, *The City of God*, (New York: The Modern Library, 1950), Book X, 3.
2. David Hesselgrave, "World Evangelization by the Year 2000?," *Mission Frontiers*, Vol. 9, No. 12, Dec. 1987, pp. 12-13.
3. Arnold Dallimore, *George Whitefield*, (Westchester, Illinois: Cornerstone Books, 1979), Vol. 1, p. 140.

THE STUDENT'S GUIDE TO THE BIBLE

Philip Yancey & Tim Stafford

A traveller's guide to the Bible invaluable for anyone making their first explorations into biblical territory. Philip Yancey and Tim Stafford are seasoned explorers themselves, and their guide works through each Bible book in turn, helping the reader to get started.

Written in a highly-readable magazine style, **The Student's Guide** unpacks the meaning and place of each book, drawing out the story-line and giving background information on characters, events and the culture of Bible times. **The Student's Guide** is the ideal book to have open next to your Bible.

Every Bible book is given . . .
- A colourfully-written introduction, bringing the characters and events to life
- Tips on what to look out for in reading the book
- A chapter-by-chapter book outline
- A listing of the book's most important passages
- Quotes from the book

019646   Royal   96 pp

CHRISTIANITY WITH POWER

Charles Kraft

Power. Politicians crave it. Money buys it. Some people will do anything for it.

But why do we seem to experience so little of God's power in our lives? Do we think and act in ways that block out Jesus' ability to heal the sick, cast out demons and work miracles? Charles Kraft believes that many modern Christians are embarrassed and reluctant to preach a gospel accompanied by supernatural power.

Step by step, the author offers us a biblical understanding of signs and wonders. And he shows how we can break out of the confines of our Western worldview, which conditions us to fit God into a predictable mould.

020369   230 pp

Other Marshall Pickering Paperbacks

SEEING IN THE DARK

Philip Yancey

In what will surely become a classic of contemporary Christian writing, Philip Yancey tackles the crisis of faith that occurs when God seems to leave us to face our struggles alone. When we ask for guidance and it is not given; when we pray for healing and it is not granted; when we seek God's blessing and then lose the very thing we cherish—what is happening? Is God silent? Capricious? Or hiding from us? Drawing on real life examples with which we are all familiar, Philip Yancey searches for answers to questions which stir inside many Christians, yet which few would ever ask aloud. *Seeing In The Dark* finds answers to these honest questions in a number of places, but particularly in the story of Job where, eventually, the pieces begin to fall into place. *Seeing In The Dark* is ultimately a book of great comfort and confidence, showing that though God's ways are sometimes deep and unknown, we can always trust in Him.

Trade paperback 018682   208 pp

Riding the Third Wave

WHAT COMES AFTER RENEWAL?

Kevin Springer (Ed)

Foreword and Afterword by John Wimber

A unique collection of testimonies from world Christian leaders, demonstrating the effect of the Third Wave of God's Holy Spirit in their lives—testimonies of renewed power and faith.

Trade paperback 015489   192 pp